Atelerix albiventris, the African pygmy hedgehog.

AFRICAN PYGMY
HEDGEHOGS
AS YOUR NEW PET

By Dennis Kelsey-Wood
Photos By Ralph Lermayer

TS-238

Facing page: The rising popularity of African pygmy hedgehogs, coupled with their scarcity at this time, has earned fortunes for those breeders who had the foresight to produce breeding colonies.

AFRICAN PYGMY HEDGEHOGS AS YOUR NEW PET

By Dennis Kelsey-Wood
Photos By Ralph Lermayer

Distributed in the UNITED STATES to the Pet Trade by T.F.H. Publications, Inc., One T.F.H. Plaza, Neptune City, NJ 07753; distributed in the UNITED STATES to the Bookstore and Library Trade by National Book Network, Inc. 4720 Boston Way, Lanham MD 20706; in CANADA to the Pet Trade by H & L Pet Supplies Inc., 27 Kingston Crescent, Kitchener, Ontario N2B 2T6; Rolf C. Hagen Ltd., 3225 Sartelon Street, Montreal 382 Quebec; in CANADA to the Book Trade by Macmillan of Canada (A Division of Canada Publishing Corporation), 164 Commander Boulevard, Agincourt, Ontario M1S 3C7; in the United Kingdom by T.F.H. Publications, PO Box 15, Waterlooville PO7 6BQ; in AUSTRALIA AND THE SOUTH PACIFIC by T.F.H. (Australia), Pty. Ltd., Box 149, Brookvale 2100 N.S.W., Australia; in NEW ZEALAND by Brooklands Aquarium Ltd. 5 McGiven Drive, New Plymouth, RD1 New Zealand; in Japan by T.F.H. Publications, Japan—Jiro Tsuda, 10-12-3 Ohjidai, Sakura, Chiba 285, Japan; in SOUTH AFRICA by Multipet Pty. Ltd., P.O. Box 35347, Northway, 4065, South Africa. Published by T.F.H. Publications, Inc.

Manufactured in the United States of America by T.F.H. Publications, Inc.

Contents

Foreword

by Ralph Lermayer, President, North American Hedgehog Association

It was one of those lovely late afternoons that have a way of impressing themselves forever in your memory. I was on a writing assignment in New Zealand at a place called Decanter Bay. The sun was setting over the vivid blue water in the sheltered cove framed with decanter-shaped rock formations while my wife Laura and I sat on the lawn soaking in the breathtaking scene and intensely evaluating the locally made dark ale. Magically, a strange little creature waddled out of the bushes lining the lawn. With no apparent concern for our presence, it began foraging in the grass just a few feet from us. Laura and I sat mesmerized as the little brown critter wandered around the lawn with his elongated snout spending most of its time deep in the grass. Occasionally the snout would emerge with a wiggling something-or-other, and the hedgehog would point his nose skyward, showing his bright black eyes as he sent the little crawlie to its just reward. The effect was instantaneous, as it is today when anyone sees these little wonders for the first time: enchantment at first sight.

The hedgehog that we had stumbled upon was the European species, *Erinaceus europaeus*, which was first brought to New Zealand by European settlers in the early 1900s. In New Zealand and throughout Europe,

Facing page: Even in the wild, hedgehogs are fed and welcomed by civilized people all over the world. Photo by David R. Dube.

The author, Dennis Kelsey-Wood, with Spike, his favorite hedgehog.

Small hedgehogs make interesting, entertaining and friendly housepets. They are clean and can be easily trained to use a cat litter box. Photo by David R. Dube.

thousands of bowls of milk, bread, and tinned meat are set out every evening in the hope of enticing these charming insect controllers into taking up residence in domestic gardens.

That first exposure to hedgehogs was in early 1985, and as soon as we *Atelerix albiventris,* from a zoo and two others from private collectors. Slowly others were found and added to the stock at Avalon. Gathering accurate information on the care and proper husbandry of hedgehogs was proving to be an even more formidable

In the wild, or in your backyard, your pet hedgehog will be constantly in search of food.

returned to the United States, we began our quest in earnest to secure adequate breeding stock and gather as much current information on these fascinating animals as was available. That proved to be a far more complicated task than we had imagined; both hedgehogs and information were hard to come by.

Intensive searching produced one pair of African pygmy hedgehogs, task. There was simply no accurate or reliable information to be had.

Slowly our library grew beyond the brief reviews of Walker's and Grzimek's works to books written in Moscow in 1909, British preservation pamphlets, and the occasional scientific paper originating from a biologist or zoo. As the limited documentation came together, only one clear fact emerged. Nobody knew for sure how to raise hedgehogs! Captive animals were being fed widely varying diets and were housed under very diverse conditions. Some scientific papers generated by zoos recommended high amounts of vegetables in the diets while others recommended insects as the only food. Most kept focused on the animals' natural habitat, diet, and preferences and studied them carefully in captivity. Pat Storer in Texas, my wife Laura, and a handful of others across the country began carefully experimenting and investigating feeding, housing, and breeding

The spines of young hedgehogs (sometimes called *hedge-hoglets*) are very sharp. They dull as the hedgehog gets older. When frightened, the hedgehog rolls up into a ball, thus exposing its spines in a separated menace.

males and females together constantly, and all reported very low success rates for breeding. Clearly, something was amiss.

The challenge and oddness of the hedgehogs piqued the interest of a few animal fanciers across the country in spite of the lack of information and limited breeding success. The hedgehog fancy will always owe a debt of gratitude to those early questing minds. They techniques. Slowly the secrets of *Atelerix albiventris,* the African pygmy hedgehog, were revealed.

Light cycle, temperature, and nutritional requirements began to emerge as crucial factors. Breeding techniques, housing, and the need for early frequent handling soon were better understood; slowly the captive breeding success began to climb.

Much of the printed data available was found to be absolutely wrong. Scientists had simply reported on the animals' behavior under the conditions in which they chose to keep them, not what the hedgehogs preferred or even required. Many of the dietary recommendations were soon proved incorrect—in some cases even detrimental to the animals' health. The hedgehog might survive on those diets but would not thrive or reproduce. Males housed with the females at birthing time would devour the offspring immediately. Breeding success rates may have been higher than figures indicated, but the young were consumed within hours, so the breeders never knew it.

The timing of this breeder education was extremely fortunate, because in 1990 the United States Department of Agriculture (USDA) banned all imports of hedgehogs from Africa for both health and political reasons. Fortunately for all of us, a couple of shipments entered the United States just prior to the ban. In spite of the limited survival and generally poor health of those animals shipped from Africa, enough were secured to adequately broaden the gene pool and to ensure successful breeding and the long-term success of the hedgehog as a pet. Through proper nutrition, veterinary care, and judicious breeding, the United States herd is now considered the healthiest in the world, and American breeders are shipping hedgehogs overseas with regularity.

Much has changed since those early years, including the formation of the North American Hedgehog Association (NAHA) in 1992. This group of hedgehog breeders and fanciers includes many of the original early breeders and is dedicated to the health and happiness of hedgehogs and the success of concerned, ethical breeders.

When the hedge-hoglets are about 5 weeks old, the mother teaches them to forage for food.

Introducing Hedgehogs

To the people of Great Britain, mainland Europe, Africa, and Asia, the hedgehog is as familiar as is the skunk to an American, or the kangaroo to an Australian. In the US and are, how they live, and how they are best cared for. It is hoped that this work will provide this information, thus helping to fill the present void in pet literature on the subject.

The young hedge-hoglets are taught to forage as soon as they leave the nest.

Australia, the hedgehog is not found as an indigenous species. However, even where it is a very common animal seen plodding across a garden in search of food, the local residents rarely have any real knowledge of what sort of creature it is. Today, more and more people, especially in the US, are keeping hedgehogs as pets.

There is a need for books that are devoted solely to these fascinating mammals and that explain what they

ANIMALS WITH SPINES

Many people, seeing a hedgehog picture or a living example, assume that the hedgehog is probably related to other spiny animals that may be more familiar to them. The porcupines of the Old and New Worlds, the Australian echidna (spiny anteater), and the spiny bandicoots of New Guinea all possess sharp spines. But they are not related to the hedgehog. They are simply examples of how quite different animals

The natural enemies of hedgehogs are birds of prey like eagles, hawks and owls. The hawk, shown to the right, has claws (talons) strong enough to pierce the hedgehog's armor.

Large owls also have strong talons which can pierce a hedgehog's armor. They readily feed on hedgehogs in their natural habitat.

ancient lineage and are considered by many scientists to be closely related to humans, surprising as this may seem.

The closest relatives of hedgehogs are the gymnures, or moonrats, and the solenodons, none of which possess spines. These perhaps bizarre-looking critters, with long snouts and tails, resemble a hedgehog without its spines.

There are some 390 species of insectivores; and of them, 18 may be called hedgehogs. Popular in children's books and folklore, the hedgehog is named for its habit of waddling slowly along hedgerows and similar places in search of food. It always seems to be eating; and as it often gives out a series of low grunts as it

have evolved a similar means of defending themselves against predators. This is one form of what is called convergent evolution. That these animals are not actually true relatives (only inasmuch as they are placental mammals) is readily apparent when many features are considered.

The porcupine is a rodent, while the echidnas and bandicoots are marsupials—there is even a spiny rat (a rodent) that is known as the thin-spined porcupine. The hedgehogs are members of a group of animals (an order) known as Insectivora. These animals share a very

Kids and hedgehogs go well together. With gentle handling, the hedgehog will soon adopt your family as its own. Children must be taught to treat the hedgehog gently and safely (for both of their sakes!).

moves around, the term "hog" was applied to it. It is not, of course, in any way related to pigs! Unlike the barbed spines of porcupines, the spines of hedgehogs, while being quite sharp, are not nearly as dangerous. They are not barbed and do not shed as do those on the tail of a porcupine when it is threatened. In fact, with care, you can easily lift up a hedgehog even when it has rolled into its famous defensive ball.

THE HEDGEHOG AS A PET

The hedgehog makes a delightful little pet because it is not an aggressive animal and makes few demands on its owner. Even wild specimens, as people living in Great Britain well know, will readily become quite tame if fed each day. However, such animals can never become as tame as will a youngster bred in captivity. Indeed, it is vitally important that captive-bred hedgehogs come from carefully bred lines. Otherwise, they will tend to roll up into a ball at the slightest disturbance. Hedgehogs have no body scent of any significance. With patience, they can be house (toilet) trained, and they make no noise other than a few clicks and grunts.

Unlike other recent exotic pets such as the potbellied pig, the hedgehog can live a very healthy and happy life even within the confines of

possible that as these insectivores become more popular, mutational color and pattern forms will appear. Already, albinos,

Even though hedgehog legs appear very weak and under-developed, they are aggressive and successful climbers.

a high-rise apartment. It will never offend your neighbors—but it will certainly fascinate them if they see it. Already, in the form of the North American Hedgehog Association (NAHA), there is a national (indeed, international) club devoted to the hobby needs of these little pets. No doubt, in the very near future, you will be able to register and exhibit your hedgehog, so they really will become the new pet on the block in a grand manner.

Hedgehog colors, while basically being mixtures of brown, black, and white, can exhibit considerable variation. Some are very light; others are almost black in appearance. Given this fact, it is entirely

creams, and patterned coats (the spines are modified hairs) are available. They will add even greater interest to the hobby once their genetic base is carefully studied. By crossing mutational forms, additional color shades can be created.

At this time, the most readily available species is from Africa; but others may start to appear more regularly on dealers' lists if they prove to be as tractable as the African pygmy hedgehog. There will be a need to establish breeding stocks of the different species because, if the history of other animals is repeated with hedgehogs—as it surely will be—the time will come when a number of species will not be readily available, if at all. Restrictions will be applied by countries where hedgehogs are indigenous.

Already, one species (*Atelerix frontalis*) is regarded as threatened, due to its popularity as a pet, and as a food delicacy in South Africa. It is hoped, therefore, that a number of pet owners will become reputable breeders so that domestic stock becomes more available. This reduces the need to take individuals from the wild.

will also rise. This is another reason why you need a pet or breeding stock from a sound source.

Hedgehogs are not especially long lived (around four to six years on average), but there is little doubt that the captive age potential of these animals will become longer as they become more established under domestic conditions. In the wild, most species hibernate during the colder months; this applies even to those living in the semi-tropical areas of our planet. Under the more controlled

Domesticated hedgehogs quickly make themselves at home as most owners allow them the run of the house.

At this time, these pets are very costly. Of course, as more breeders become established, so will the prices fall; but as this happens, the number of poorly bred individuals

conditions of captivity, hibernation may not occur. It may be that this may reduce their lifespan. A period of estivation (dormancy), therefore, may be of benefit to pet hedgehogs; but as yet, this fact has not been established. There is thus still much to be learned about these animals. This helps to make them both adorable yet challenging to those for whom they have appeal.

The ability of the hedgehog to camouflage itself in its surroundings is its first line of defense against predators.

SPECIES COVERED

In this work, I have chosen to describe all of the hedgehog species, not just those which are presently the most popular. This gives you a much broader background to your new pet. Data from one species may well apply to another, or at least provide clues to

unanswered questions on the lifestyle of those kept, but which have not as yet been fully studied. The text also covers the Madagascar (now the Malagasy Republic) "hedgehogs," even though there is little chance that you will ever be able to own any of the species from that country. These species, also known as tenrecs, are not in the same family as the typical hedgehogs, but are very similar in appearance and are close relatives. It was therefore felt that for completeness, they should be included so that you are aware of their existence.

Lifestyle of Hedgehogs

The more you know about the lifestyle of any animal in the wild, the greater your chances of caring for it successfully under captive conditions. This is especially applicable to any attempts to breed a given species. Very often, an animal can be maintained quite happily under domestic conditions, yet it may never breed. This is usually because one or more crucial aspects of its lifestyle are not being considered. Such needs may not seem important to us, but to a hedgehog they may make the difference between being willing to mate and rear babies, and not being willing.

Likewise, elements that are missing within the diet or within living conditions will greatly affect the ultimate lifespan of an individual. Hedgehogs are relatively new pets, and there is much that is still not known about them, even in the wild. This may seem surprising with such well-known mammals, at least to Europeans. Yet the very fact that an animal is so common can often result in it's being somewhat ignored as a study subject.

Some subspecies of hedgehogs are already disappearing within their home ranges; some are thought to have vanished already. Within this chapter, I have summarized as much general data as possible on the lifestyle of hedgehogs as a group of species. Where appropriate, individual species and any peculiarities or special needs they are known to have are cited.

Hedgehogs can be very friendly. Kids love to play with them, but they must understand their respon- sibilities. If this hedgehog were to fall to the floor, it would probably be mortally injured!

DISTRIBUTION AND GENERAL HABITATS

Hedgehogs probably evolved in Europe, spread to Asia, and later to Africa. Presently, they are found as far north as about the 60th parallel, which means southern Scandinavia to southern Siberia and northern Mongolia. South of the equator, they have colonized as far as about the 30th parallel, or South Africa. Their most westerly distributions are Mauritania in North Africa; to the east, they are found as far as northern China. They are absent from Australasia and the New World.

In Malagasy (Madagascar), they are seen in the form of the tenrecs. These animals have developed uniquely ever since that large island became detached from Africa millions of years ago. They are examples of parallel evolution. This means animals with common ancestors that have been separated in time for thousands of years yet, because of similar ecological conditions, have continued to develop similar phenotypes (appearances) and physiological traits with other species derived from the same shared ancestors.

Hedgehogs inhabit areas that comprise any of the following: grasslands, savanna, light forest, scrub, deserts, and cultivated areas. Some are found in marshlands, but most avoid such habitats. The streaked tenrec is unusual in that it is quite at home in dense rain forests, as well as in the more open terrains popular with most hedgehogs. A few species are actually extending their areas of distribution; others are being restricted as a result of habitat destruction for roads and other human activities. However, many hedgehogs, with their low-profile existence and insectivorous diet, have

If your hedgehog escapes, he might head for cover. They especially like woodpiles because there are natural caves and sympathetic coloration which aids their camouflage.

been able to adjust quite well to the close presence of humans.

The fact that they will eat many creatures not liked by humans, such as insects, baby mice, snakes, and lizards, often helps their cause with humans, who are usually happy to allow them to remain in gardens and on cultivated lands. In some countries, hedgehogs are still regarded as a food delicacy; but in Western Europe, this is largely a thing of the past. The same is true of their former use in the preparation of all kinds of medicines that were held to cure just about every human ailment in past centuries.

HEDGEHOG HOMES

Hedgehogs take advantage of whatever cover they can in order to provide themselves with somewhere to sleep for a night. This will be in the form of piles of leaves under which they can bury, crevices in rocks and, in those species that live close to humans, under sheds and similar places. However, all hedgehogs can dig small burrows. These burrows are used as nesting sites for pregnant females to bear their young and as places in which to hibernate if this is appropriate because of colder winter periods. The burrows are not very long: they are just long enough for the hedgehog to crawl in and curl up into a ball in order to avoid predators and escape the heat of the midday sun. They are widened at the end when a female is bearing young. The streaked tenrec (*Hemicentetes semispinosus*) is known to

Hedgehogs eat insects and other foods of vegetable origin. This animal is eating the roots of a grass.

develop quite extensive tunnels that are communal for a number of individuals. The streaked tenrec is one of only two species that appears to cohabit with its fellows, the other being the dwarf tenrec (*Echinops telfairi*). The common tenrec (*Tenrec ecaudatus*) excavates a quite long burrow, up to six feet, and plugs the opening with soil once it has entered for the hibernation period.

HIBERNATION AND ESTIVATION

Hibernation is a survival strategy used by many animals, including hedgehogs, to overcome the problems that would otherwise be created if they had to remain active and search for food when the weather is very cold. This would necessitate using up valuable energy, the source of which—food—is difficult to come by. Estivation, or torpor, is similar to hibernation but not as intensive. It is a natural rhythm of some animals during warmer weather, occurring when conditions are not good and food is scarce. In the colder more northerly parts of their range, hedgehogs hibernate; but in southerly ranges, they will tend to estivate. During hibernation, a hedgehog's heartbeat rate drops by nearly 90 percent, an immense savings on energy needs. In order to survive the hibernation period, which may be for a number of months, hedgehogs eat as much as they can so that they have goodly fat layers, which are the source of their metabolic energy needs during their big sleep.

Under artificial conditions, such as when you keep one of these animals as a pet, it may not hibernate at all. You will be providing warm quarters and a regular supply of food, thus overcoming the need to enter a deep sleep. To what degree this affects longevity—and breeding potential—has not yet been thoroughly studied. Hedgehogs will normally look for a mate shortly after coming out of hibernation.

Physiological changes that occur during hibernation prepare the hedgehog for the next period of its life. If the hibernation period is absent, this may affect the individual's urge to reproduce. However, once the individual has adjusted to this change in its natural annual rhythms, it may then be willing to breed if all other conditions are suitable. This is why in many wild-caught animals it may take some time—years in some instances—before the individuals will breed.

Subsequent generations may be more willing to reproduce because they are "less" wild. Hormonal changes in their body, over many generations, change their physiological make-up—they are becoming domesticated.

Hibernation may last from just a few weeks to six months, depending on the severity of the winter within the individual's home range. In temperate climates such as Great

There are cages made especially for small animals like the hedgehog. These cages are easily cleaned and are roomy, with lots of ventilation. Most petshops carry such cages. Photo courtesy Rolf C. Hagen Corp.

Hedgehogs love woodpiles. Their natural hiding places, the fact that insects crawl around them, and their colors, all add to the reasons why hedgehogs like them.

Britain, many parts of the US and Canada, and mainland Europe, the hibernation months will be from October to about March. They correspond to

hedgehogs)—Mostly nocturnal and crepuscular. This is the genus of the little hedgehog that is the main subject of this book.

Paraechinus (desert

Mother hedgehog teaches her babies how to forage. This instruction begins after the babies leave the nest, normally when they are about five weeks old.

the warmer periods in the most southerly parts of hedgehog ranges.

ACTIVITY PERIODS

Hedgehogs are, in the main, nocturnal in their habits. They usually start to move around at twilight and may still be active as dawn approaches—these periods being known as crepuscular. The activity periods of the various genera are as follows:

Erinaceus (European hedgehogs)—Mostly nocturnal, but may be crepuscular and even, on occasion, diurnal (active during daylight hours).

Atelerix (African

hedgehogs)—Mostly nocturnal, occasionally crepuscular.

Hemiechinus (long-eared desert hedgehogs)—Strictly nocturnal.

Tenrec (common tenrec)—Nocturnal and crepuscular.

Setifer (setifer, or large Madagascar "hedgehog"). Strictly nocturnal.

Hemicentetes (streaked tenrec)—*H. semispinosus semispinosus* is both nocturnal and diurnal, according to local conditions. *H. s. nigriceps* is strictly nocturnal.

Echinops (small Madagascar "hedgehog")— Nocturnal and crepuscular.

Under captive conditions, hedgehogs will modify their activity periods within reason. This is done so that activity periods will coincide with feeding times. However, in an outdoor situation, they will not wish to move around during the daytime on hot days. Rather, they will venture forth once the sun is past its peak.

FEEDING HABITS

Most hedgehogs are omnivorous, meaning they will eat foods of both animal and plant origins. But they display a strong leaning toward being

Hedgehog food includes most invertebrates, such as insects, spiders, earthworms, larvae, and even scorpions in the case of desert hedgehogs. Frogs are another item of the diet. They will eat "pinky" (hairless newborn) baby mice and rats, as well as small snakes and lizards. Chicks that have fallen from their nests, as well as the chicks and eggs of ground-dwelling avians, are other favored items. Carrion will also be eaten, which indicates that the hedgehog is very much an opportunistic feeder. Fruits, seeds, and vegetables make

Some hedgehogs scour fallen trees, searching for ants and other crawling insects.

carnivorous and insectivorous . The Asiatic desert hedgehog appears to be wholly carnivorous/insectivorous, while the tenrecs are nearly so.

up the main part of their limited plant-matter diet.

Hedgehogs do not tackle any large prey because they are not fast enough to hunt such animals down.

Even with relatively weak-looking legs, the hedgehog can climb trees unless it is overweight and obese.

However, they have been known to attack small poisonous snakes. One account cited that a hedgehog approached a viper and promptly rolled itself into a ball. The snake struck at it a number of times, badly injuring itself in the process. Tired and weak, the snake attempted to crawl away; but the hedgehog then attacked it, pinning it down with its front claws and lethally biting into its neck. When attacking scorpions, the hedgehog is astute enough to bite off the scorpion's tail sting first!

The hedgehog is, conversely, food to other animals. Among its most dangerous enemies are the fox, birds of prey, and even rats. Even its defensive posture of rolling into a ball is not always sufficient protection from a determined predator. Rats will bite away the spines of young hedgehogs in order to get at a vulnerable spot. Foxes have been known to carry the hedgehog to a shallow stream and drop it in so that it is forced to swim for air, when it can be attacked. A hedgehog forms itself into a defensive ball by means of the longitudinal muscles that run around the edge of the spine belt. These muscles act like a drawstring that pulls the skin around the sides so that it really is a tight little ball of spines. The spines can be moved individually by a complex muscle system beneath the skin. This muscle system allows the spines to face the direction that a predator is trying to attack.

The typical dental

formulas of hedgehogs are as follows: i 3/2 , c 1/1, pm 3/2, m 3/3 = $^1/_2$ jaw = 36. They may differ somewhat from one species to another. In reading the dental formulas, the following are their meanings: i = incisor, c = canine, pm = premolar, and m = molar. The information in front of the oblique line applies to the top jaw; that behind it refers to the lower jaw. For example, i2-3/3 means that there are two or three incisors in the top jaw and three in the lower jaw. This method of display is standard in all mammals.

SELF-ANOINTING

A somewhat peculiar habit of hedgehogs is that related to what is called *self-anointing*. Certain substances found on its travels elicit the hedgehog to lick the substances until they form a frothy saliva. This is then deposited onto the spines of each side of the body. Some experts believe that the purpose of this action is part of the hedgehog's mating ritual— maybe it acts like a perfume to attract members of the opposite sex! However, others feel that it is part of the hedgehog's defensive strategy because these animals have been seen to rub against toads, whose secretions are known to be noxious at least and poisonous at worst to other animals.

As toxins are being mentioned, it can be added that hedgehogs are remarkably resilient to many poisons. For example, some toxins strong enough to kill a man, and even a horse, appear not to unduly bother these little animals. This said, there may be

Many farmers and others use poisons to rid themselves of rats, mice and other disease-carrying mammals. Fortunately, hedgehogs are almost immune from many toxins that would affect a horse or human.

others that they might quickly succumb to so you must *never* take chances and leave any disinfectants and the like near your pets.

SOCIAL LIFE

For the vast majority of hedgehogs, there is little or no social life. They are very much creatures that are quite happy with their own company. Of course, they come together in order to perpetuate the species, but that is it, other than in two species of tenrecs, which will tolerate their own kind out of the breeding seasons.

Hedgehogs are not territorial in the sense that they defend fixed areas of land, but they keep their distance from each other. Generally, based on one study, the distance that these animals keep from members of the same sex is about 60 feet. When males, in particular, do meet in the search for willing females during the breeding season, the result is very fierce fighting until the loser retreats.

Females under captive conditions are more gregarious with their own kind if they have plenty of space. But the problem is that if one of the females should have babies, the other will readily cannibalize the litter if she possibly can. Also, even if two females appear to be getting along fine, it may happen that one day some little source of contention triggers them into fierce fighting. Serious, even fatal, injuries can be the result. Close confinement of these pets together is therefore definitely not recommended.

Even though your hedgehog is well fed, he will keep foraging for food. Hedgehogs easily become obese.

VOCALIZATIONS

Hedgehogs are capable of a range of sounds that indicate their mood of the moment. When under threat, some will hiss and make a clicking sound, while when hurt or under attack, they emit a high-pitched squeal that cannot be mistaken for anything but fear and pain. When feeding, they issue a steady series of grunts that range from a sniffing sort of sound to an obvious pig-like grunt. An extra sound that at least one species of tenrecs makes is stridulation. This is created by the vibration of the spines against each other, much in the way that porcupines do. It is thought to be a means by which a female can call her offspring. In other hedgehog species, stridulation may be practiced at a lower level of audibility, so it is not so readily observed by human onlookers.

HEDGEHOG SENSES

It is generally felt that hearing is the hedgehog's prime sense. This is probably followed by its sense of smell, with eyesight being adequate rather than exceptional. The position of the hedgehog's eyes are such that it has a good field of vision, and sound binocular vision at short distances. Its hearing will most certainly cover high frequencies so it can pick up sounds emitted by insects. Any animal with an elongated snout has a keen sense of smell because such a conformation allows for many thousands of receptors within the mucous membranes of the snout. These same membranes also serve the purpose of heating cold air and cooling warm air as it passes along the sinuses of the muzzle.

BREEDING

Female hedgehogs may (in the wild) have one or two litters per year. Mating usually takes place a few weeks after the hedgehogs have awakened from their period of hibernation. The time of mating is, for most hedgehogs, the only time that these animals socialize. It is preceded with much grunting and other noises, as well as with some head butting. After mating, the two hedgehogs go their separate ways. The female prepares a nest of leaves in a shallow burrow, and there the babies are born. They remain in the nest for the first four to five weeks; then they will accompany the mother on foraging trips. They are weaned when about six weeks of age, when they become independent and wander away from their mother and siblings. In some instances, youngsters may remain together for a week or two before leading their solitary lives.

Female hedgehogs in the wild usually have one or two litters per year; after mating, the male and female separate and may never meet again.

Hedgehog Housing

There are no commercially made homes especially designed for hedgehogs at this time because they are such a relatively new pet, but pet shops stock housing units (designed for other kinds of animals) that can be suitable for your hedgehogs.

crucial to the success of your hedgehog as a pet. In any case, even if it is allowed freedom for long periods, it is best that you can restrict its movements whenever necessary.

If you are handy and have the time and inclination, you can construct a housing enclosure, but it is far

The female is brought to the male's quarters for breeding. Estrus is induced upon exposure to the male rather than on a standard cycle. This feature allows these normally solitary animals to successfully breed during chance encounters in the wild.

THE HOUSE HEDGEHOG

You can let your hedgehog roam freely around your home, but it is advisable to restrict its movements during its first week or two with you—until it is at ease in your presence. This also enables you to check that it is eating satisfactorily, and better facilitates the bonding process that is going to be absolutely

more easier and practical to purchase a commercially made unit. This enclosure should be a minimum of 122x91cm (4 x 3 ft.), with a minimum height of 46cm (18 in.). The enclosure can be made by stapling 19-gauge wire mesh onto a 5x2.5cm (2 x 1 in.) framework. The hole size of the wire mesh can be 2.5x2.5cm (1 x 1 in.). In order to make the unit easily transportable, each of the four panels can be hinged.

The enclosure can then stand on a wooden base that fits snugly inside the framework. This will give stability to the unit. You might also fit a retaining board along the inner edges of the wire framework or on the outer edges of the floor. This retaining board, which need be only about 7.5cm high (3 in.), will help to prevent the floor-covering material from spilling out of the enclosure. Within the enclosure, you can provide a small nestbox that is somewhat longer, wider, and taller than your pet. The entrance hole should be large enough for the hedgehog to fit through easily. Hedgehogs enter their burrows head first and exit in the same way,

so they must be able to turn around inside with no problem. If the hedgehog is a youngster, do make allowance for its growth. If a floor is included in the nestbox, make sure that it can easily be detached for ease of cleaning—the simplest way is if it or one of the sides is hinged.

The floor is best painted with a gloss finish so that it is easily wiped. It can then be covered with newspaper and a 1 in.-layer of wood shavings. The nestbox can be lined in the same manner.

You now have a small and simple home for your new pet. Obviously, the larger the floor area of the enclosure the better. With a small unit, it is assumed that your pet will be allowed out for periods of more extended exercise when you are present to keep an eye on it.

Pet shops carry a wide variety of cages that will be suitable for your hedgehog's accommodations. Photo courtesy Rolf C. Hagen Corp.

A partial view of a hedgehog breeding room. In addition to the breeding cards attached to the front of the cages, the breeder of these hedgehogs also keeps a detailed log of all matings and the ensuing litters.

If space is rather limited, you can increase the floor area of the enclosure described by making it a two-floor home. This is done by making an upper gallery, which has one or two wooden ramps with struts across them so that your pet can move from one level to the other without difficulty. Of course, the side panels will have to be higher if a second floor is featured. You can furnish the indoor enclosure in much the same way as is discussed for the enclosed outdoor home.

Offering less space, but a low-cost wooden option for your pet, would be either one of the rabbit hutches made for indoor use. You might also consider a double or triple budgerigar-breeder cage, which is readily available from pet shops or any company selling avicultural supplies. The triple-breeder cages have the advantage that they come with removable sliding partitions that double as extra accommodations if you should want to house an extra hedgehog at short notice. These breeder cages and rabbit hutches come unpainted, so they will need good protection with washable paints.

Another form of indoor housing is to use a medium-to-large fiberglass carrying case—the kind used for cats and small dogs. These carrying cases come in a wide variety of designs. Fiberglass has the great advantage that fleas, lice, and the like do not like

this material because they cannot easily hide and breed in it like they can in the crevices of wood. It is very easy to thoroughly clean. A carrying case is always useful to have, even if you use alternative accommodations. It can be used to transport your little pet to the vet, to the homes of your friends, on vacations, and so forth. It also makes a useful breeding box—but do be sure it is of a goodly size.

A variation on the fiberglass theme is a large tray that has a covering of sturdy wire mesh. Be sure that it is deep enough so that the spines of your pet do not touch the overhead wire mesh. Again, you should provide a nestbox or similar darkened retreat.

An aquarium tank is another potential hedgehog home that is easy to clean and offers good security. However, it should be of a large size, and certainly large enough to accommodate a sleep box or nestbox so that your pet can retreat from bright lights if it so wishes. (An alternative to a nestbox is a large-diameter piece of PVC tubing, fitted onto a plastic base so that it remains stationary.) The aquarium unit should be at least 62x31x31cm (24 x 12 x 12 in).

In each of these confined accommodations, do bear in mind that they should represent places only where your pet can sleep and stay for short periods. It is very important that your hedgehog is allowed out to roam freely in your home, or certain rooms, and not be a virtual prisoner of a small container. Continual confinement will stress any animal. In laboratories, the life expectancy of such animals may be only 50 percent of that which can be expected for a pet given lots of room in which to exercise, explore, and live. In any case, a pet kept under close confinement is hardly a pet and will never display its potential as will one that is treated as a member of the family in every way.

OUTDOOR ACCOMMODATIONS

Some hedgehog keepers opt to house their pets in an outdoor facility, be it a garden shed or similar building, or a suitably sized enclosure. Before even considering this housing option, you must be mindful of the following, all of which can have a direct impact on the welfare of your pet: 1) a hedgehog (whether housed outdoors or indoors) needs protection from direct sunlight; 2) uncontrolled temperatures and harmful fumes such as those that occur in garages present obvious health risks; 3) hedgehogs can fall prey to a number of different animals; and 4) there are, unfortunately, individuals that might try to steal your hedgehog(s) as an easy way to make money.

If you cannot provide accommodations that will prevent problems associated with any of the above, do not keep your hedgehog outdoors.

Planning the Outdoor Home

If an outbuilding is used, it is still preferable to have

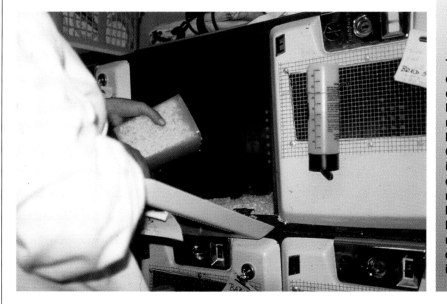

The open cage contains a litter of newborn hoglets. Clean litter is provided daily to minimize bacteria levels and reduce the chance of infection.

a small external run attached to it so that your pet can venture out on warm nights and enjoy the natural feeling of fresh air and even light rain. Cut a small entrance to connect the shed to the enclosure. The enclosure must be covered with sturdy wire mesh so that there is no risk that predators could gain entry and try to make

31cm (12 in.) back toward the inside of the shed. Fill in, and this should prove to be an adequate safeguard. The same applies to the perimeter of any outdoor enclosure that is not on a solid (concrete or slab) base.

The floor can be covered with a generous mixture of wood shavings, dry-leaf litter, and branches of

At the present time, color marking is the accepted method for animal identification.

a meal of your little friend. What you must ensure is that the shed is on a solid base; otherwise, the hedgehog may burrow under the sides. If the shed is not on a solid base, you can do the following:

Dig a channel around the inside of the building to a depth of about 31cm (12 in.), and a width of the same dimension. Place 62cm (24 in.) weldwire in the channel and bend

conifer trees. This will provide the sort of terrain that hedgehogs like best. Periodically, the floor covering should be cleaned out and replaced. You may also use some peat or potting soil, either of which is preferred to garden soil. A suitable nestbox can be included. If the nestbox is to be placed in an outdoor enclosure, be sure that it is made of at least 2.5cm (1 in.)-thick timber that has been previously treated with a suitable preservative. An indoor nestbox can, of course, be made from less stout wood.

The outdoor enclosure can be made using 2.5 x2.5cm (1 x 1 in.) wire mesh fencing. That which is covered with green epoxy resin or PVC looks very stylish but is, of course, more costly. If you use

aesthetically pleasing for you and your family. Hedgehogs are passable, if not brilliant, climbers. With this in mind, you can place a number of large rocks so that they provide something upon which your pet can clamber. A few stout, lengthy logs strategically placed (and secure) can provide archways. In an

This pregnant hedgehog is being checked for mites and other external parasites.

galvanized wire, the best thing to do is to paint it with bitumen. This will make it less readily noticed and greatly extend its life. The height of the enclosure should be about 93cm (36 in.).

Furnishing the Outdoor Home

You can make your pet's home more interesting for your pet if you add a few decorations, which will also make it more

outdoor enclosure, one or two small shrubs will provide sites for the hedgehog to sleep under during the day if it does not wish to use its nestbox (which it might not use anyway if good natural alternatives are at its disposal). Large-diameter sewerage pipes or PVC piping will make nice hideaways. A large enclosure can have turfs of grass laid.

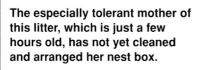

The especially tolerant mother of this litter, which is just a few hours old, has not yet cleaned and arranged her nest box.

Small secure hiding places need to be provided with any kind of housing. Hedgehogs will retreat to them for sleeping and security.

One way or another, there is no need to make your pet's home a boring enclosure or shed that has had no imagination applied to its design. Do not forget that even if outdoor space is limited, you can still construct a two-story home that will provide plenty of room for your pet. Use good thick timber and treat it with a preservative. You can then furnish the upper level as well as the one below. The connecting ramp should be of a gentle slope and wide enough so that your pet will have no inhibitions about using it.

FOOD CONTAINERS

You will need two containers for feeding, one for food and one for water. They should be shallow and heavy—those made of crock (earthenware) being the best. In an outdoor enclosure, you could provide a *shallow* garden bird-bath type concrete or plastic water bowl. It can be fitted so that it is flush with the surrounding ground and makes a nice-looking water receptacle.

Indoor units can be fitted with small gravity-fed water bottles of the size sold for rabbits. They are clipped to the outside of the cage, and their

Your hedgehog's food bowl should be sturdy and easy to clean. Photo courtesy Rolf C. Hagen Corp.

spout passes between the wire to the inside. This way, it is easy to refill them. However, until you are sure that your pet knows how to use the water bottle, be sure to include a regular open water vessel. Invest in a quality bottle because the cheaper models tend to drip and soak the floor substrate near them.

LITTER TRAYS

You will need a litter tray for your indoor pet. Hedgehogs are very clean little animals and will by choice prefer to soil a designated area rather than foul their nesting and feeding areas. The litter tray size should be 15x45cm (6 x 9 in.) minimum, with sides no less than 7.5cm (3 in). You might cut the opening down to 5cm (2 in.) so that it is easy for your pet to enter. Plastic is the best

material because it is easy to keep in clean condition, but do replace it whenever scratch marks are seen. They provide homes for pathogenic (disease-causing) microorganisms. It might be worthwhile bonding the litter tray to something heavy, or placing it into a floor-mounted retainer;

Breeding quarters must be precisely regulated for temperature and ventilation.

Cat litter can be used in your hedgehog's litter box. Be sure to change it on a regular basis. Pet shops stock a variety of cat litters. Photo courtesy Rolf C. Hagen Corp.

The hedgehog to the immediate right is obese. The hedgehog to the far right is of the proper weight. Animals that are overweight will not breed successfully, as their body is telling them to prepare for hibernation.

otherwise, your pet just might tip it over when it moves in or out.

With regard to the litter substrate, those produced for cats is acceptable, but some of them are rather dusty and can also represent a health problem to hedgehogs. This is because the teats and penis of these animals, as well as their anal regions, are so close to the floor. Damp litter grits may compact onto the anus, while minute particles may create irritation to the penis of the male or teats of the female. The natural plant litter now available for cats is better because it is entirely biodegradable after use. Alternatively, potting soil is clean and soft. Avoid sawdust

because, like grit cat litter, it can cause irritations. Wood shavings are not very absorbent, but if deep enough, and cleaned regularly, they will work.

The litter tray should be placed as far from the food containers as possible—which is not very far in a small carrying case. This is why the preferred hedgehog housing is an indoor enclosure. Place a little of your pet's fecal matter into the litter tray, then clean the rest of the floor covering and replace. This way, your pet will be attracted to the scent of its fecal matter and hopefully start to use the litter box. The very act of using its little toilet will become what is known in psychological terms as an internalized reinforcer. However, once your pet has become familiar with its litter tray, it is important that it is kept clean. No animal wants to wade through its own excrement in order to attend its needs!

HIBERNATION

If your hedgehog is kept indoors during the winter months, it will probably not hibernate. If it is outdoors, it will seek a suitable site and enter its long winter sleep. But do remember that the African pygmy hedgehog, which is the species that you are almost certain to obtain, is not a species from cold climates. It should not be left outdoors in temperate winters. If it is, it may not be physically able to hibernate through a long winter as can its Eurasian cousins. It might pass straight from hibernation into hedgehog heaven! This species should be hibernated (if at all) in a cool outdoor shed or its like so that you can bring it out of hibernation after about four to eight weeks. This is done by *slowly* raising the temperature a degree or two over a two-week period, or until the pet starts to move around. It enters hibernation when the temperature reaches a given low. If this is to be attempted with your pet, it must be done slowly, just as it would under natural conditions. Sudden temperature fluctuations are not healthy for any animal.

In warmer winter climates, the hedgehog must be provided with at

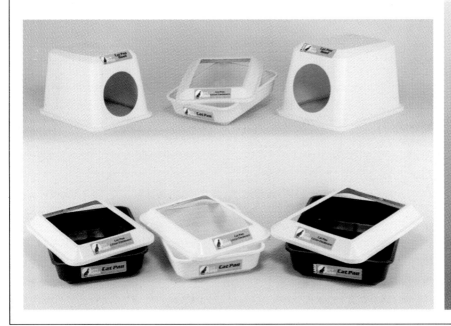

Plastic litter boxes are lightweight and easy to clean. Photo courtesy Rolf C. Hagen Corp.

least one or two sites from which it can choose. Be very sure that nesting sites are higher than the flood level, so there is no risk that if there is a heavy rain, this might result in the nesting chamber or box becoming flooded! If need be, build up the earth so that this risk is removed.

Place the entrance so that it is not exposed to the cold winds and rain.

will be able to forage for food. Of course, in your back yard this is not a consideration, but is a point of interest.

If your pet goes into a short hibernation, do not disturb it. During warm breaks in a short winter, it may awake and venture forth but should not be given regular feeds at this time. It can be given about 20 percent of its normal

Hedgehogs experience a rapid rate of development. These babies are just five days old.

Interestingly, some hibernating animals actually prepare their winter quarters to face the worst weather. The reason is that they instinctively know that this will be the last side of the mountain, or wherever, that will be clear of snow. This means that, when they awake, if the immediate area is clear of snow, so will the rest of their range be, and they

diet. It will then have minimal food in its digestive tract should the weather turn cold again. But it is stressed that while a short period of estivation may benefit a hedgehog, full-blown hibernation is not desirable in those species that are native to equatorial regions.

If you live in a year-round, mild-to-warm

At six weeks of age, the hoglet's eyes are open; they are eating solid food and are ready to be weaned.

climate, the main consideration for the outdoor pet is that it does have optional sites that are well shaded, and from which it can escape the hot rays of the sun. Hedgehogs are basically nocturnal animals and are not happy being left in exposed situations from which they cannot retreat. Their preferred temperature range is 65-80°F (18- 26.7°C). As it falls below 45°F (7.2°C), the hedgehog may become more torpid in preparation for hibernation, depending on the chill factor. Stay within the safe range.

HEDGEHOGS AND OTHER ANIMALS

Where hedgehogs are concerned, other animals come in two kinds: those that are potential

These young hoglets are being weaned. A weaning pen like the one shown here allows careful monitoring of the hoglets to ensure proper food and water intake. Frequent handling at this stage creates happy, trusting pets.

At birth, the spines of a normal-colored hedgehog are white, which changes to brown or black as the animal gets older.

Opposite page: It is easy to distinguish between male and female hedgehogs. The sheath of a male's penis looks like a belly button.

predators, and those that are not. Dogs and cats are natural predators of these pets; but if brought up with them, they very quickly get on well together. The spines of a hedgehog are ample protection from the over-inquisitive dog or cat you may already own. Other pets in the household quickly learn to leave the hedgehog alone. Ultimately,

the hedgehog becomes just another animal that your pets see moving around the home. They may even share a dinner plate with this strange spiny resident, depending on the nature of the dog, cat, and hedgehog.

However, it would be prudent to monitor affairs during the early days of introduction. A medium-

The spines of a hedgehog grow very rapidly. This hoglet is just a few hours old.

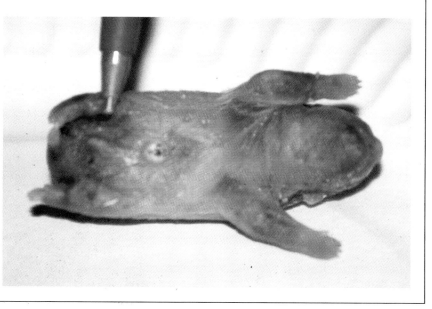

Hedgehog babies can be handled when they are about three weeks old.

The mother of these hoglets developed mastitis, which is an inflammation of the mammary glands. This condition necessitated handrearing. Success with handrearing is often limited, and so it should be attempted only in really desperate situations.

to-large dog might pick up the hedgehog and carry it around like a ball, dropping it every now and then. It may also paw at the hedgehog. We owned such a dog, who would delight in bringing us wild hedgehogs that wandered into our large garden. Thankfully, he eventually got bored with this amusement and left the hedgehogs to go on their way undisturbed. If you own one or more pet ferrets, be advised that they are not good companions for hedgehogs and are best kept apart. Ferrets are more adept at getting a hold on the hedgehog because they are much lower to the ground than dogs or cats.

If you have foxes or coyotes in your area, it would be wise to make your outdoor enclosure in the style of an aviary, so that there is no risk that these predators could scale a low fence and try to carry off your pet. Non-poisonous snakes are not a problem to hedgehogs, who might just decide to make a meal of them if they attempted to mess with these little insectivores.

Poisonous snakes are another matter, though generally they will avoid hedgehogs, and definitely so if they have ever attempted to bite one and ended up on the end of a face full of spines! You may be told by uninformed people that hedgehogs are immune to the bites of venomous snakes—this is not true. They have a greater capacity to survive bites, but they are not immune. They are also able to rapidly lower their head and spine defenses against striking snakes; thus, they very often walk away without injury.

New weanlings learning to make a living with mom.

Make sure that your other household pets are properly introduced to your pet hedgehog. All but the

most aggressive will give the spiny newcomer a wide berth.

Choosing a Hedgehog

Before you go about the process of selecting and purchasing your hedgehog, your first consideration must be whether these pets can legally be kept in your state and, indeed, in your locality. In the US, each state has its own regulations. You can find out about them from your local vet, who, if unsure, will give you the address or phone number of the local USDA office, which will advise you. In Britain, the indigenous species *Erinaceus europaeus* cannot be taken from the wild and kept or offered for sale. Pet hedgehogs are, therefore, imported species.

At the time of writing, the situation in the US is as follows. You cannot keep or breed hedgehogs in the following states: California, Alaska, and Arizona. Colorado is presently undecided. It may be kept in any of the other states. What you should ascertain is that there are no local bylaws prohibiting these pets—this is unlikely, but it is always wise to check with your town hall. In the US, the hedgehog is classified as an exotic species. This will not change because none of the species are indigenous to the US.

Pet shops are able to sell this pet without having to obtain a permit from the USDA because it is classified as a non-dangerous pet. As a pet owner, you are not required to be licensed; but if you decide to become a breeder and sell your surplus

Use non-toxic paints to identify the weanlings for lineage and sex.

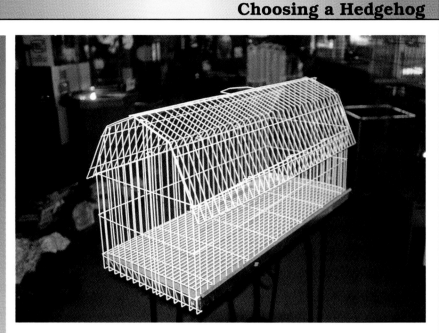

This type of cage is adequate for a non-breeding pet hedgehog. Set up with a few rocks, a sleeping hole, and a water bottle, it will keep your pet safe and happy.

offspring, you are. This is federal law and you should comply with it. If you keep a hedgehog in a state that forbids it, you can be arrested, and your pet confiscated. You are ill advised to break the law, and are better counseled to try and contact other would-be owners and form a petitioning group to see if the pet can be reevaluated. You may also find that the North American Hedgehog Association may be able to help by furnishing advice that will prove valuable in your petition. One final comment on this subject:

Unlike other more common pets that are more tolerant of noise, a female hedgehog that has been bred must have quiet seclusion.

the fact that a local pet shop may be selling hedgehogs does not mean that they can be kept in that locality, so do check the situation out *before* you purchase.

Assuming there are no legal restrictions, your next step is to prepare the hedgehog's accommodations. This is the logical sequence of events. But it is surprising just how many people will

selection may not be extensive, because they are a rather new pet in the US, and are no less so in Great Britain. The majority of those available, if of the species *Atelerix albiventris* (African pygmy hedgehog), will have been bred in captivity. Imports from Africa have now ceased, so any further imports will be of Eurasian species whose suitability as pets has not yet been established.

Early and frequent handling is required to develop a people-friendly disposition in your hedgehog.

purchase a pet on impulse. If purchased on the spur of the moment, then you have to provide makeshift accommodations, which are often inadequate for the pet. So, you immediately start off on the wrong foot.

Assuming you have attended to these matters, you should try to see as many hedgehogs as possible. The available

The more individuals you can get to see the better you are able to develop a mental image of what a nice young example should look like. Color should not be a factor of any great importance to you, though in reality it often is to pet owners. Most species are within the range of browns, with some black and white in the coat and spines. *Health and*

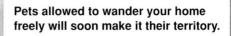

Pets allowed to wander your home freely will soon make it their territory.

This is a perfect example of self-anointing. When a strange smell or taste is encountered, a hedgehog may begin to foam at the mouth and then go through strange contortions to spread the foam over its back. The reason for this behavior is unknown.

temperament are by far the most important criteria when assessing pets. Any unhealthy pet totally spoils for you what should be an exciting and fun-filled time. Instead, you will be worrying over your pet, and the hedgehog is a pet on which our knowledge of its ailments and treatments is limited at this time. If it has a poor temperament, all it will do is curl up into a ball every time you approach it—hardly what you are expecting of a new family member.

WHAT AGE?

You need a young individual because hedgehogs are not long-lived like dogs and cats. Once mature, it is impossible to ascertain age accurately. These pets are weaned from their mother at about four to eight weeks of age. By then, they are eating independently, so this is the ideal time for you to obtain one. It is important that they have been fully weaned. With this in mind, the eight-week-old baby is better than one of five to six weeks. They will look like small versions of the adults. It is fine to obtain one that is a little older as long as it is seen to be friendly. Likewise, the would-be breeder may prefer to purchase an older pair.

WHICH SEX?

Hedgehogs are solitary animals so your pet hedgehog should be housed singly in its accommodations. This being so, the choice of sex is really immaterial; both will make fine pets. Of course, if you wish to attempt breeding, you will want one of each sex.

ASSESSING HEALTH

When purchasing any pet, your first observations as to the likely health of it should be in respect to the conditions under which it is living. If they are cramped, dirty, and smelly, this should be sufficient to see you beating a hasty retreat.

The modern pet shop should have hygienic caging in which the residents have clean floor covering, clean and well-filled water dispensers or pots, and probably some food left in their food dish. If you are satisfied on these points, you can commence evaluating the hedgehog. A good pet shop will not, of course, knowingly offer an unwell pet for sale. Even so, you should be able to assess health because you are going to have to do this once you become the new owner.

EYES: They should be round, dark, and clear. They should be neither weepy nor partially closed if the pet is awake.

NOSE: It should be dry to just moist, showing neither any suggestion of discharge nor any signs of being swollen.

EARS: They are short (except in the long-eared desert species) and erectile. They should be neither dirty (from brown wax) inside nor offensive in smell.

FUR: The underbelly should be soft and in no way should look dry and out of condition. Part the fur to see if there are any visible signs of ectoparasites (lice, fleas, or ticks). Lice are a gray color and move slowly, fleas are red-brown and move quickly, ticks yellowish and buried head first into the skin). Their fecal matter is seen in the

More than likely, your pet hedgehog will never pass up a tasty tidbit.

form of clusters of tiny black-red specks. Fleas tend to congregate near warm areas, which are behind the ears, under the arms, and around the base of the tail. Part the spines just as you would the fur in order to see whether there are any signs of parasites. If spines are seen to be shedding, this is a sign of ill health. These pets do not shed spines if they are healthy.

SKIN: There should be neither bald areas of skin

problem to the hedgehog, as long as the wound that caused it has cleared up totally. An indoor pet, which does not have the opportunity to use its claws as it would in the wild, may need its claws trimmed periodically so they do not become overlong. Your vet will attend to this for you, or show you how to do it if you decide to purchase your own nail clippers (the guillotine-type clippers are the least costly, and very

Choose a pet with natural curiosity, bright clear eyes, and a willingness to open up to new people.

nor any signs of swellings, abrasions, or red areas devoid of fur. The body should be plump and feel as though there is sufficient "substance" to it.

Feet: They are small and have five digits on each foot. Inspect the pads, which should feel soft, but firm, on a youngster. A missing digit is not a matter of any great

good on small mammal nails).

ANAL REGION: If you can, try to inspect the anal region below the short tail to see that it is neither clogged with hard fecal matter nor showing signs of staining that results from diarrhea.

GENERAL: If the hedgehog is moving around in its cage, stand and watch it for a few minutes. It should move without any signs of problem, such as a limp. It should not continually be scratching itself, coughing, or vomiting. Its breathing should be steady, never wheezy, labored, or gasping, all of which indicate respiratory problems. Note whether the fecal matter on the cage floor is firm, not liquid or streaked with blood.

Assuming all of that discussed checks out just

the sort of conditions you might keep it under.

QUESTIONS TO ASK

The most important question you need answered is about the diet the seller is presently feeding to the hedgehog, and how long the animal has been receiving it. It is always wise to try and maintain the same regimen during the initial move from the pet store to your home. At such times pets do become stressed,

Hedgehogs bred from quality stock and handled frequently at weaning age soon become acclimated to their new environment and become very tractable pets.

fine, you can assume that at that moment at least the hedgehog is in sound health. Some dealers may give you a limited guarantee as to health, but you should not expect one automatically. After all, once the pet leaves their premises and care, they have no way of knowing how you will look after it, or

especially as they have already gone through two or three transportations (breeder to wholesaler to dealer) in their short lives before you obtain them.

What they now need is a little stability, and this commences with their food. If the diet has been very basic, then you can immediately commence widening the variety—but still supplying whatever the dealer has been feeding as basic rations.

THE MATTER OF TEMPERAMENT

Temperament, which for our purposes we will restrict to tractability, is the visual expression of two important pressures. One is the genetic base of the

primary cause. The most important thing is that you *do not* obtain a pet with a questionable temperament.

How do you decide whether or not a given individual has a good nature? This is not so simple with a baby, but very easy with a mature specimen, so we will discuss the latter first. If it curls into a ball and makes a

Allow the potential pet hedgehog a few minutes to open up when it is first handled.

individual; the other is the environment, which includes everything from living conditions to temperature and feeding to handling. Very often, it can be impossible to determine whether bad temperament is the result of poor breeding (genetic) or inadequate bonding (handling), or both. For the hedgehog pet owner, it matters little which is the

clicking sound when approached, this indicates fear. It may also hiss and attempt to bite. It will spread its spines to face in all directions in order to protect itself. Further, when touched, it will "hop" upward about $1/2$ inch. This is sufficient to dissuade any potential aggressor.

If it is not quite so nervous, it may uncurl and cautiously sniff the air and your hand. It may still be on guard, and this is indicated by the snout being lowered and the spines being brought forward over the crown to provide protection to the head as it begins to proceed forward. If it becomes frightened, it will hiss and snort, thrusting its head forward.

A pet that is well imprinted on humans will,

TAMING A HEDGEHOG

A baby will often be rather apprehensive and display the signs just described, depending on just how much time the breeder had devoted to socializing it. With a youngster, however, it takes little time to win it over as a pet. What the author does to befriend new arrivals (mature or youngsters) with

A hedgehog that will not unroll from the balled-up, defensive posture will not make a very good pet.

of course, not curl up and will happily allow you to hold it. The individual that stays in a tight ball and resists all attempts to persuade it to show itself is not going to be an easy specimen of which to make a delightful pet. When a hedgehog is relaxed in your company, its spines will not be erect, but will lay flat against its body.

belligerent natures is as follows. They are placed into a large cage and allowed a nestbox for one or two days. The nestbox is then removed so that they cannot take a defensive posture and hurl vocal abuse at us from within! At the same time, we allow them the freedom of a room in which to waddle about. When in this situation, they are far less aggressive and more amenable to being lifted up. You might need to wear thick gloves to remove them from their cage the first few times; but you may find, from the outset, that you can lift them up from the floor without gloves.

Repeat this for two or three days, and you will then be able to lift the pet from its cage without problem. The nestbox can be returned once your pet will leave it when you call its name or tap its food dish (assuming it is awake). It is best to tame a pet in the early evening when it is wide awake, rather than to disturb it during the day. Once you can handle your pet, it will become more and more friendly. Be aware that it will lick your fingers and may even nip them initially.

Nipping should cease once the pet is friendly and has learned that your fingers are attached to the rest of you and are not food items! All baby animals (including humans) will nip as part of their learning process, so you should not regard this as an act of aggression.

HEDGEHOG PRICES AND BUYER PROBLEMS

At this time, hedgehogs are quite expensive little pets. Good examples of colors, such as creams or whites, will command higher prices; mutational colors or patterns, as they arrive, will be even more expensive. However, as the hedgehog becomes bred on a larger scale, the prices will naturally begin to fall. Exactly where they will level

A hedgehog should be held in a secure but gentle manner.

It took this little hedgehog about ten minutes before it relaxed and uncurled completely.

off, and how long this will take, is always a speculative question with a new pet. Even as the prices fall, quality offspring will command a higher price.

One of the problems with new exotic pets, and which you should be made aware of, is in respect to the dispersal of inferior animals. When a new pet arrives on the scene, there is naturally a much larger demand than there is a supply. This keeps prices at a high level. The most desirable hedgehogs will be females with good breeding records, and prepotent males. Breeders will tend to keep the best of them (if they are wise) and sell that stock which is not perhaps quite as good. The stock that is sold becomes the pet hedgehogs.

As the market gets larger, there are more breeders

and, as always, there are those who breed only for the money, regardless of the quality of their stock. If a male or female turns out to be less than a capable producer, or produces unhealthy or inferior stock, they will sell it as a pet, or palm it off as a good breeding animal to the unsuspecting novice. Because of their value, even terrible little monsters will still be sold by some breeders who give no thought to the damage these animals may bring to the hobby as a whole.

Some pet owners will start to breed inferior animals in the hopes they can cash in on the new pet. Very soon, problems start to appear in the species. These breeders will sell stock at much reduced rates when compared to those of reputable breeders.

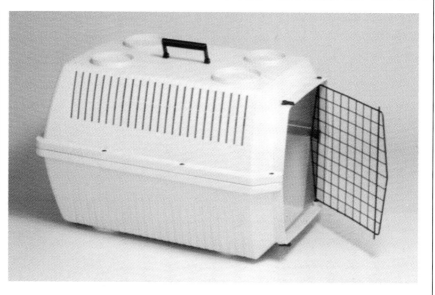

Unfortunately, this downward spiral in respect to quality and temperament is inevitable and has happened in every single pet species you could name. As a first-time owner, you will have to be cautious to avoid being sold an inferior animal in such a young hobby. What you can do is insist that your pet comes complete with a current health certificate.

Do bear in mind that many of the people breeding and selling hedgehogs at this time had never even heard of this little animal a year or two ago, let alone knew all about it. The limited gene pool from which the present pets have come means that low-grade temperaments, in particular, will be a major concern over the next few years. You must, therefore, be prudent in your choice of pet and insist that it

displays a tractable nature. Do not allow yourself to be sold a pet unless you can see clear evidence that it can be handled without remaining in a defensive position.

Do not purchase breeding stock unless you are totally satisfied that it comes from a very reputable source, who will ideally maintain breeding records that you can examine if you so wish.

TRANSPORTING YOUR HEDGEHOG HOME

The best way to transport your newly acquired pet to its new home is via a pet carrier that has a generous lining of wood shavings (pine is preferred—avoid red cedar) and fresh alfalfa hay. If the journey is short, then no food or water will be needed. On longer journeys, you could scatter some dry cat chow in the box and maybe include a few small pieces of apple, which will provide adequate moisture. (A water vessel would no doubt be tipped or would topple over.) Do make the journey without stopping to show friends your new pet—they can see it later when it has settled in.

BUYING VIA MAIL ORDER

More people are conned when buying via mail order than when they are buying direct and can see what they are handing over their hard-earned money for. Here are a few tips that may help you avoid problems.

1. Pay via credit card if you can. This at least gives you some comeback on the seller if you are not satisfied.

2. Have a written contract before you part with your money. Inform the seller exactly about what you want in respect to age, sex, color, tractability, and health certificate. Have the seller confirm by letter or fax that this is what is being supplied and that live delivery is guaranteed. If the seller is unwilling to do this, then you should be wise enough to look for another source.

3. If in doubt, contact the NAHA, which may have some input on the seller, or of disreputable people. Already, some agents have taken deposits on stock that they cannot supply and then conveniently moved elsewhere when the going gets hot!

If you are paying for costly breeding stock, the seller should confirm their status. This means that if

Your hedgehog can be an enjoyable little pet, and younger members of the family can actively participate in caring for it.

you are buying a pair of hedgehogs, you will receive one of each sex, not two hedgehogs of the same sex! You need to know if they are proven breeders or not, meaning that each has produced viable offspring. If possible, you need to know about their breeding history (age, number of litters, number of offspring per litter, colors produced, and any problems experienced). A reputable breeder has nothing to hide and will gladly supply all data. Any buyers that rush into the purchase of breeding stock and then find that they have been sold a lemon really have only themselves to blame.

ON ARRIVAL HOME

Once at home, you should place your hedgehog in its accommodations and provide both food and water for it. Do not interfere with it or let children start picking it up right away. It needs time to explore its home, eat, and have a rest. Just carry on as normal and it will steadily become familiar with the noises and activities that will become part of its new environment. Do not introduce it to other resident pets at this time, as this will merely place unnecessary stress on it. But do keep an eye on it to see if it is eating or not.

The following day you can start the process of bonding with your pet. Do this by offering it tasty morsels from your hand. At first, it may be rather apprehensive and roll into a ball at your approach. But this behavior will stop as it realizes that you mean no harm to it. Being a youngster, it will

Even though hedgehogs are fairly good climbers, they should be supervised when they are climbing around from any great heights.

A cardboard tube such as the one shown here can make a cozy, secure retreat for a hedgehog.

more quickly settle than had it been an adult. But even mature hedgehogs that have had little or no contact with humans can become tame in a remarkably short time if they are well bred. Before you know it, your pet will let you scratch its chin and underbelly, and will be happily taking treats from you.

Hedgehogs and other insectivores are not the most intelligent of animals, so they do not compare with dogs or cats in this area. You cannot teach these pets to do party tricks and the like, nor are they easily house trained. Their charm lies in the fact that they can become very friendly and confiding little pets, they are quiet, and, in the right environment, can be quite amusing.

A baby hedgehog (a hoglet) can be rested on its back in the palm of your hand and will study you as you study it. Within a day or two, it will be happily waddling around your home in search of little morsels of food in the form of insects and their like. When other pets are introduced to it, always monitor their interactions. Never leave medium-to-large dogs alone with your new pet until you are quite sure that the dog is very familiar with the hedgehog and has no malice toward it.

The time to be especially watchful is when the dog is eating and the hedgehog approaches its dish. Most dogs are rather possessive about their food and their playthings. You cannot force animals to be friends with each other, but you can be on hand to intervene if things start to get a little aggressive. Other pets will

This hedgehog's accommodations are rather small. To compensate for this, the owner of this animal makes sure that his pet is allowed out for daily exercise.

Many hedgehog owners let their pets have the run of the house and let them return to their cages at will. The hedgehogs soon learn to make themselves quite at home and will turn up in the darndest places!

In the wild, a hedgehog might clean out the small area under this plank for a comfy home. When winter comes, he will cover the entrance with dirt for a snug winter hibernation.

ultimately ignore the hedgehog, become friends with it, or make it quite clear that it is not welcome near them.

You must not discipline a dog that clearly does not like the new family resident. Bear in mind that the hedgehog is to the other pets an interloper competing with them for food and your attentions. Do not give them reasons to become jealous of the hedgehog; instead, do quite the opposite. Give resident pets extra attention so that they can see that they are not losing out to the newcomer. Eventually, the resident pets will probably just ignore the hedgehog. They will come to find out that it is well equipped to defend itself by rolling into a ball of spines.

HEDGEHOGS AND VETS

It is advisable that you take your new pet for a veterinary checkup once it has settled into your home and is happy to be inspected without taking up its defensive posture—the tight ball. At this time, few vets will have had any practical experience with these animals, especially in the US, where the species is not indigenous. Once your vet knows you have one of these pets, he may seek out data on them for future reference on the assumption that more of these animals will be making visits to the clinic, which will be the case as they become very much more popular.

Mealtime for this hedgehog. Providing a proper diet for a hedgehog is a fairly simple matter.

Your pet shop can supply you with all of the equipment that you will need for your hedgehog, including

gravity-fed water bottles, which can be seen on the display rack above.

Feeding

The diet of the wild hedgehog is so cosmopolitan that these pets are simplicity itself to feed. You may attempt to duplicate what hedgehogs eat in the wild, but this is not essential. There are plenty of alternative foods that will be readily taken and that will provide less of a health risk as a bonus. (Consider that foods gathered from the wild may contain the eggs of parasites and other pathogens. Further, the cultivation of live foods is a messy and time-consuming business.)

For all practical purposes, you may regard the hedgehog as you would any carnivore—meaning dogs, cats, ferrets, and the like. The difference is that your hedgehog may show somewhat more willingness to eat vegetable and fruit matter. It will also most certainly avail itself of any insects or other creepy crawlies that it may come across as it waddles around your home or in its outside enclosure.

For their size, hedgehogs are very healthy eaters; rarely will they turn down a food item. Of course, in the wild this is very important because they must put on sufficient weight during the season of plenty so that they can go through their winter hibernation or summer estivation (the latter being the case with the African pygmy hedgehog) without

Shown here are dry cat food supplemented with mealworms and a small treat of cottage cheese. The small portion is a normal daily ration; the large portion would be required by a lactating female with a large litter.

problems. When under controlled warm conditions, they may tend to eat very heartily during their first year, in preparation for the winter that never comes. Subsequently, they may consume less as they adapt to their metabolic needs.

However, some hedgehogs may prove to be rather picky eaters, depending on their age, how long they have been in captivity, and how they have been handled and treated. It is, therefore, a matter that is determined on an individual basis, rather than their rigidly following the generally accepted notions of their eating habits. The same goes for the items that they will consume. Each pet is an individual and subject to its own personal tastes. Its tastes are influenced by what it is familiar with from its life before you obtained it. Application of common sense is important in correctly feeding these animals.

THE ESSENTIAL FOOD GROUPS

Your pet needs a range of foods from each of the three essential food groups. These groups are proteins, fats, and carbohydrates. Each of them serves its own purpose in your pet's body. If you are aware of what they are, and of the other three components of food—vitamins, minerals, and water—you are better positioned to ensure that your hedgehog is never at risk to being fed an inadequate diet.

PROTEINS: These compounds are composed of substances called amino acids. Certain foods, such

Quality canned dog food with a good grade of dry cat food and occasional treats like cottage cheese will maintain a balanced diet for your hedgehog.

Mealworms can be purchased in pet shops. Remember, they are a dietary supplement—not a staple.

as meat and fish, are the richest sources of proteins. They are the building blocks of the body. Proteins, once eaten, are oxidized in the body and then rebuilt into the kind of tissues needed by your pet. Muscle, brain, and blood are mainly protein. If an animal is short of food, its metabolism will break down body tissues in order to convert them into energy needed for day-to-day activity. The result is the animal loses weight and, beyond a certain level, health suffers. Proteins are especially needed by growing hedgehogs and by those recovering from an illness or awakening after hibernation. They are also vital to a breeding female. All foods contain proteins in varying quantities; but

some, such as fruits, vegetables, and grain by-products, are not especially rich in them. Certain amino acids are derived only from meat or fish sources.

FATS: These substances are normally found in association with proteins in meat, but to a much lesser degree in fish and poultry. They are used to form layers of fatty insulation under the skin to help keep animals warm during cold weather. They also give food its individual taste. Fats are the first bodily tissues to be broken down when energy is needed. They are, in fact, the richest source of stored energy. Again, fats are present in most foods; but the amounts in grain, seeds, fruits, and vegetables is minimal compared to that in meat.

CARBOHYDRATES: These foods are primarily the source of energy needed for muscular activity. They also provide bulk to the diet. Composed of various sugars that are rapidly oxidized to release their stored energy, they are the most common, thus least costly, of the major foods. This is why they are used a lot in the preparation of

brain, heart, lungs, and so on. They provide the body with resistance to disease and adverse physiological conditions. If any are missing in the diet, this will show itself in loss of vigor, health, or breeding capacity. However, an excess of vitamins can be as dangerous as a lack of them, so *balance* is the all-important word where they are concerned.

The richest sources of

Regular pet-food bowls are a far better choice than are paper plates. They are more durable and economical in the long run.

prepared animal foods. Their prime sources are grain, seed, and their by-products, such as flour, cereals, and bread.

VITAMINS: These substances are not foods, but chemical compounds (catalysts) that enable food to be broken down during metabolism. They are also vital to the performance of organs such as the eyes,

vitamins are fruits, vegetables, fish oils, and liver. Some vitamins can be synthesized in your pet's body, but most have to be provided within the diet. If the diet is wide-ranging, it is unlikely that any important vitamins will be lacking. However, if your pet proves to be a picky eater, then supplements may be required on veterinary advice. They can be added to your pet's food. (It is not recommendable to administer either vitamins or medicines via your pet's water because you cannot be sure that the pet will take the required dosage.)

Whcn a pet has been ill and received medicines, it may well be that it will need extra vitamins in the form of an initial injection, followed by tablets or powders. This is because

must therefore be stored in cool, dark places in order to maintain their maximum nutritional potential.

MINERALS: These substances are elements in their various forms. Examples are copper, iron, iodine, calcium, magnesium, selenium, potassium, and many more. They are utilized in the cells of the body to give them rigidity, and in the formation of compounds

Feeders and waterers of the type used for hamsters and gerbils are perfectly suitable for hedgehogs.

only a few medicines are selective in the microorganisms they kill. As a result, they will destroy gut microflora (bacteria) that synthesize certain vitamins in the animal's body.

Vitamins are easily destroyed by heat (boiling), direct sunlight, dampness, and exposure to air. They, and any foods they are in,

that serve many other functions in general metabolism. Like vitamins, an excess or lack of them can be harmful to health. However, mineral deficiency or excess is unlikely if a well-balanced diet is followed. If any minerals are especially needed as supplements at certain times, they will be those such as calcium, which is essential in the production of milk in lactating females.

WATER: This precious liquid is, of course, vital to life itself. Animals can get by without this or that food item, and they can even get by without food for a certain period. But without water, no creature can survive for very long. All food items contain water in various quantities. It is also a by-product of digestion. Even so, to remain in what is called water balance, your hedgehog should have daily access to it.

The amount consumed will reflect the amount of water within the diet. There is not a set amount that each pet should have. Water should be fresh each day and supplied in a clean container. Some water, such as that from your faucet, may not be very appealing to drink. This is because water authorities may add all kinds of chemicals to make it hygienic. Some pets would rather drink from puddles of rainwater than from a faucet. In such instances, you can purchase untainted water in bottles. Fortunately, hedgehogs are able to obtain most of their water from their diet. As long as they drink a little, they will be fine. But do ensure that they can drink whenever they choose, which means it must be available at all times.

SUGGESTED DIET ITEMS

The so-called "complete" dry cat foods are excellent for your hedgehog. They are rich in protein and provide something hard upon which your pet can exercise its teeth. I doubt that a "complete" food has yet been produced, so do not feed your pet exclusively on dry food. Instead, consider dry food as the basic diet and supplement it with other items.

Good-quality canned dog or cat foods are fine. They have been fortified with vitamins and contain various amounts of protein. The more costly brands will have more meat in them; the economy varieties will contain a higher percentage of carbohydrates. Canned cat foods are invariably richer in proteins than are dog foods. The quantity of protein and other contents are listed on the label.

Raw butcher's meat is another fine protein source for a hedgehog. It is also a useful food to give for jaw/muscle exercise. Be sure that it is fit for human consumption. Chop it into suitably small pieces. You can also feed cooked meats, and you can give meat on the bone. I would advise against letting your pet eat rabbit and poultry on the bone because the bones easily splinter, but the meats themselves are excellent. Boiled fish is another useful protein source, but not raw fish, which contains a potentially dangerous constituent that is removed only by cooking.

Scrambled or boiled egg will be well received, as will cheese, both being excellent sources of protein. You can purchase frozen invertebrates such

is not important that such foods are offered live to your hedgehog.

Some hedgehog owners do feed maggots to their pets; and if you decide to do likewise, a word of caution is appropriate. Maggots are associated with botulism in birds and mammals. The thin black line seen in these creatures is the source of the problem, so do not feed

Your hedgehog's foraging activities will be a source of delight to you.

as worms and insects from your pet shop or aquatic dealer. When thawed, these items make valuable, tasty treats for a hedgehog. They are virtually free of any risk of pathogens (disease-causing organisms) and thus far safer (and more convenient) than those gathered in the wild. You can also obtain from the same source various live worms and insects, but it

maggots until the line has disappeared. Keep maggots in sawdust prior to feeding so they will void their toxic contents into it. Better still, ask yourself if it would not be wiser to leave them out of the diet, even though the hedgehog has a high resistance to many toxins. Why take chances? There are plenty of other good foods such as mealworms and frozen crustaceans.

Extra carbohydrates (additional to those in dog and cat foods) can be given via porridge oats or similar breakfast cereals, or bread, in milk.

In regard to fruits and vegetables, the best thing to do is to make a small sliced salad of them and see which your pet shows a liking for. You can add a few nuts and cereal grains. Any fruits and vegetables will be fine. If your hedgehog shows little initial interest in these vitamin-rich foods, do not despair. You can add a couple of drops of cod liver oil or something similar to the meat and carbohydrate part of the diet, and this will provide many vitamins.

Continue trying the fruits periodically because some animals are rather seasonal in when they will take certain items. At the same time, your pet may never have been offered these foods before, so it needs to get a taste for them. An alternative way of offering new foods to your pet is by preparing moist or dry mashes. You can use something like a breakfast cereal, mixed with bread crumbs as the base item.

Now add chopped boiled egg, bits of meat, thawed deep-frozen invertebrates, cheese, diced fruits and vegetables, and maybe some seeds or nuts. Moisten (do not make this sloppy) with either a drop of tepid water, beef broth, or something similar, and thoroughly mix before feeding. You can make a quantity that will last for three or four days and store it in the refrigerator. The recipe can include all kinds of things, including honey and milk. However, when milk is added to anything, do bear in mind it quickly sours, so add it only as you are about to feed your pet. Honey is very nutritious, but it can attract bees and wasps during the warmer months. These creatures could inflict a painful sting on a hedgehog, so this item is best fed during the colder months. There is no need to feed your pet chocolate or any other kind of sweet, other than an occasional bit of honey or maybe a cookie or two.

Never be afraid to experiment in the feeding regimen because the wider the range of food the better. But do apply common sense in the choice of items, and do make notes on all the foods that are accepted. This information may be useful later on, to you and to other hedgehog owners.

WHEN TO FEED AND HOW MUCH

Hedgehogs are opportunistic foragers, which means they spend much of their time ambling along and taking whatever food they come across as they travel. They, therefore, prefer to have a number of small meals rather than one large one. However, like most animals, they will adapt to whatever feeding schedule you are able to organize. Given that you may have to go out to work, you should try to feed them three meals per day. One before you leave,

work a little for their food—by scattering dry cat chow around their enclosure or pen. This simulates their natural habit of utilizing their nose to seek out food items. It provides excellent psychological therapy for them, as it helps to relieve subconscious stress that is often the main precursor of health problems.

With regard to the amount of food to give them, this is not always

Agouti is the coloration most commonly seen in pet hedgehogs.

one at lunch, and one later in the evening. Since hedgehogs are more active in the evening, the evening meal should be the main meal of the day—with the midday meal being the one that can be dropped if required (but increase the quantities of the other two).

You can certainly make things a little more interesting—and have them

easy to gauge in any animal that is a continual browser and that has a body covering (in this case of spines) that masks the true state of its muscles. But essentially, when turned on their back, their underparts should display good substance. Their eyes should be sparkling, and their fur should look in fine condition, not dried or lacking life.

Your other guide is by ensuring that at any one meal they do not eat it all. Initially, give them a good helping. When they have eaten enough, they will start to show disinterest and walk away from their dish. Assess how much has been left and reduce this amount at the next meal. See how things go. If they eat all of their food, give them more until they are satiated. Over the two to three daily meals, or however many you are giving them, you will by this method establish approximately how much they require each day. Bear in mind that a young hedgehog will require more food per day as it grows. This state will persist until it is physically mature, which will not be until it is about six to twelve months of age.

Food-intake needs are influenced by the ambient temperature, the activity level of the pet, its age, health, and individual appetite. It is also influenced by the quality of the food. If the quality is high, then less will be eaten than if it is of items containing poor nutrients, when more will be required to meet bodily needs. Remember also that a lactating female may eat five to eight times her normal rations.

The pet hedgehog can and, if allowed, will gain weight rapidly. Its metabolism is designed that way to allow it to prepare for hibernation in the wild. Do not allow your pet to become overweight.

OBESITY AND THINNESS

It is a little more difficult to assess obesity in hedgehogs than in dogs or cats, for example. This is because hedgehogs have a predisposition toward autumn fatness. This is quite natural for any hibernating species. This does not mean balloon-like! If you feel that your pet is a little too rotund, reduce the quantity of each meal—not the makeup of it. In this way, no important ingredients will be left out.

If the reverse is the case, you must increase quantities and check that the quality of the food is good (meaning enough proteins in particular). It might also be prudent to consult your vet. Your pet

A hedgehog foraging and feeding in the wild.

may have a problem that is restricting its ability to digest its food properly, so is not getting full benefit from what it eats.

OBSERVE EATING HABITS

Very often, the first signs of an impending illness are seen in the form of a reduced appetite, or an excess or lack of thirst. Unless you have devoted some time to the feeding habits of your pet, you will hardly be familiar with these signs. Note which items are greedily devoured. They will be important in tempting the ill patient into maintaining its food intake. If a normally healthy eater suddenly shows scant interest in its food, this will be for a very definite reason and should prompt you to try and find out what it is before things deteriorate.

You should also be familiar with the fecal state of each pet. A healthy hedgehog voids moist but firm torpedo-shaped pellets that are a dark color. If they become green or liquid, there is a problem. This may only be minor— maybe an excessively liquid diet—but it might be the first sign of internal disorder, or a more serious condition. Act promptly and consult your vet.

If you find that your pet is showing total disinterest in its food, you can usually tempt it with live invertebrates. If they fail, you can assume that your pet is not well, or that the ambient temperature is too low and the pet is about to become torpid. Raise the temperature a few degrees per day and see if this brings about a change. At the same time consult your vet.

If you have the absolute trust of the mother, then early handling of the hoglets will ensure the docile nature that it takes to become good pets.

Practical Breeding

Although hedgehog species have been bred for a number of years under captive conditions, they cannot be regarded as "established" in the same way that most other pets are. Whereas the mere presence of a sexually receptive female is usually enough to prompt breeding in dogs, cats, rabbits, guinea pigs, and other pet mammals, the same is not quite so true with hedgehogs. In this area of their lives, they may be better compared with some of the exotic birds that require particular conditions to be just right before they will readily reproduce and rear their young.

This said, long-established breeders such as Ralph and Laura Lermayer, Pat Storer, LaDonna Stage and others have now developed very successful herds to a number of generations. Their pioneer work means that tractable females are now available, which are very different from the early imports in respect to their breeding qualities. Even so, the nature of hedgehogs is such that it is extremely important that great attention is given to the conditions under which they are bred, and to the genetics of their breeding. If these matters are not carefully monitored, you can expect to have problems in due course.

BREEDING CONSIDERATIONS

Although the breeding of any animal species is an

Close-up of an adult hedgehog's spines. This is the most commonly seen coloration in *A. albiventris*. Photo by Michael Gilroy.

This hedgehog weanling is being marked for its sex and the litter from which it was produced. This is a very simple procedure.

exciting and fulfilling area of keeping pets, it is not without its drawbacks. Many pet owners fail to fully appreciate that breeding is not something that should be undertaken lightly. It implies a great deal of extra responsibility on the part of the owner. The female is totally dependent on the owner to provide the things that she would normally provide for herself in the wild. That is, food, a place to have her babies, and the general safe conditions that must prevail once the offspring are born.

Once the youngsters are weaned, they will be able to stay together only for a short while. This is for two reasons. One is that hedgehogs become sexually mature at a young age. If they are not separated into groups of the same sex, they may commence breeding, which is not desirable in such young stock. Further, the males will start to quarrel and maybe fight.

You must, therefore, have the facility, from the outset, to provide extra housing for the sex groups. If they are not sold or given to friends while they are still young, you may be faced with the possibility of having to accommodate them in their own individual housing. It is true that they can be kept in one group in a very large enclosure while young, but there is then the very real danger that they may fight quite savagely without having given previous indications of their intentions.

The prudent would-be breeder will, therefore, take these realities into consideration and have the facility to accommodate a number of hedgehogs. If these matters are attended to, it will make your breeding program more streamlined and enjoyable.

Assuming that you are prepared to invest whatever is needed in preparation for breeding, you should next be aware of what you are up against from a practical viewpoint. Also, you should understand at least the very basics of genetic principles that will be essential in developing a herd of successful hedgehogs.

BREEDING CONDITION
The term *breeding condition* embraces many facets of an animal's makeup. They include both its physical condition and its mental state. The former is more readily achieved, and under your direct control, than the latter. Your pet must be neither overweight nor underweight, obesity being

Prior to both breeding and giving birth, the female hedgehog should be inspected very carefully, especially in the area of the mammary glands.

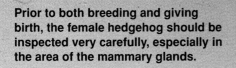

far more dangerous to a breeding female than if she is on the slim side. It can take months to slim an overweight hedgehog down to hard fitness. Never think in terms of quick breeding with such a pet. In fact, overweight females will usually prove to be non-breeders.

Even if she is able to breed, an overweight female is at increased risk

On the limited data available, it seems that the male's reproductive capacity peaks while he is 12-18 months of age. Thereafter, his ability to service as many females in a given time span as he did at his peak starts to decline. But this does not appear to affect his ability to sire litters of good size.

The mental state of the female is much harder to

Gender—this is a male—and the umbilical area are very pronounced at birth.

that she will have problems during the births. It is as important that the male is a fit specimen because this affects his ability to mate properly with his partner. It may also affect the vigor of his sperm, thus the potential litter size. The age of the breeding pair, as well as the ambient temperature at the time of fertilization (the mating), can also affect litter size.

assess because very many factors may influence her instincts. Breeding may be divided into two parts as far as the female is concerned. One is her willingness to be mated in the first place; the other is her ability to have a litter, then rear it. If she is not fit and well fed, she may be disinclined to mate. There is then the matter of compatibility with the male. Little is known about this side of the hedgehog, but we can assume that not every male will appeal to every female. Indeed, there is evidence that this is so, but it is apparently not a factor of any great importance at this time. Most females appear to be quite cosmopolitan in the choice of partners. There is no evidence of bonding, so the female's sex life is a

stressed or fearful of anything in her immediate surroundings. This may happen in any case with a maiden female, though subsequent litters may be reared with no problems.

Cannibalism is not uncommon in wild hedgehogs and was evident in early domestic breedings. Its incidence has declined sharply with the establishment of captive-

Spines are present at birth, but they are covered by a thin membrane to ease the birthing process. This membrane dries and shrinks within hours, allowing the spines to protrude.

series of one-night stands!

Assuming she has been mated, she may abort a litter if her environment is not to her liking. She must have one or more nesting sites at her disposal (depending on the size of her accommodations) that satisfy her need for a quiet and safe place for the births. Once parturition has taken place, she may kill her offspring if she is

bred herds. This was to be expected for numerous reasons:

1. Captive-bred females are less stressed by their restricted environment than are wild-caught individuals. They become more at ease in the company of humans. With each successive generation, the stress levels drop—assuming that attention is given to the quality of breeding.

2. As feeding techniques improve, there is less risk that an important dietary deficiency could be the source of the problem.

3. Management techniques—meaning attention to light, temperature, and other environmental factors—have been given more attention, thus reducing stress-factor-related cannibalism.

SEXING HEDGEHOGS

Hedgehogs can be sexed by inspecting their underbelly and ano-genital area. The female (a sow), has five pairs of mammae. Her vulva (urogenital opening) is relatively close to the anus. The penis of the male (a boar) is partially pendulous and directed toward the front of the body. Unlike its position in dogs, cats, and other pets that you may be familiar with, it is much more forward—toward the mid-belly region. The sexes can be distinguished when only a few days old, so this should be no problem for you by the time they are weaned, which is when you will be obtaining, at the earliest, your first pets.

BREEDING AGE

Like many other mammals, hedgehogs reach sexual maturity at a very young age. This may be only shortly after they are weaned, which is why such hoglets should be separated into sex groups once they are feeding independently. It is very unwise to breed any animal that has not reached full physical maturity. It places great physiological, as well as psychological, pressure on them. Wait until the female is about six months of age. The male may be a little younger if you wish to test him on a proven female.

It is always sound strategy to mate unproven youngsters to proven adults. This makes the mating process easier for the youngster, while removing one element of doubt from a situation in which no offspring are forthcoming.

SELECTING BREEDING STOCK

At this time in the development of the hobby, there is really not a great deal of difference in the quality of hedgehogs in respect to their conformation. This will become a factor once inadequate and unskilled breeders start to get to work on the matter! Where care must be exercised is in the selection of stock that has a good breeding record for vigor, litter numbers, parental care, temperament, and general health. Each of these factors is of immense importance to any potential breeder who wishes to build a reputation as a quality breeder.

Indeed, at no time in the future should these factors ever be sacrificed for whims of fashion that

lines, or you can purchase from two or more breeders. The potential breeder should obtain as much background information as possible on potential breeding stock.

The age at which you purchase breeding stock will have some considerable influence on the price. Obviously, young hoglets are rather less costly than

These two hedgehogs are about to be bred. The female is the larger of the two animals.

are related to conformational changes, which has sadly happened in so many other pets once they become very popular.

Considering the exceedingly limited gene pool from which the first few pets have developed, it is wise to try and obtain unrelated males and females. A registered NAHA breeder keeps different

mature individuals. Likewise, proven adults are more costly than unbred mature specimens. The problem with youngsters is that you must first wait until they mature before you can breed them. Even then, you cannot be sure whether or not they will prove to be sound breeders.

With an adult specimen, you at least know what it has matured to look like, so this aspect is not an unknown. You can breed it quite quickly and, therefore, will be gambling only on its ability to reproduce good stock. This will be less of a gamble if it has come from a well-established line.

Sometimes, beginners like to purchase one or more mated females. This is not advisable with these pets.

You must be patient, take things one step at a time, and progress only based on your practical knowledge of keeping hedgehogs. With regard to the number of individuals that are suggested as a small breeding nucleus, it would be wise to have one boar and two or three sows. Actually, the boar can be omitted if there is a breeder

The more a young hedgehog is handled, the better a pet it can become.

The gestation period is only about 35 days. To move a hedgehog during this short period can only result in stress and the risk of birth problems. In any case, a novice doing this will have no practical experience in even caring for hedgehogs, so will hardly be in a position to adequately look after pregnant sows and their subsequent litters.

of repute within driving distance of your home. This keeps costs down and will give you more flexibility to experiment with different boars during your early days. If you invest in a boar, you will be very tempted to use it on all of your females—yet it may not prove to be a good breeder, or it may transmit problems.

Select the boar with the utmost care. Although he has no more influence on the quality of the offspring than does the sow, both contributing 50 percent of their genes to their offspring, his elevated position in breeding programs is because he has a much greater potential to spread his genes through a population than does any one sow. He can be mated very many times in a year, whereas the sow is limited in the number of litters that she can have. All too often, novice breeders (and some old hands who should know better), rush to use a given famous boar for no other reason than that it is famous. This is seen in dogs, cats, horses, and so on. Such a policy is actually often quite ridiculous because the use of such a male may serve no realistic purpose. Indeed, it may result in a drop in the average quality of offspring. But this is another story and beyond the scope of this book. What you should ensure is that the boar complements the female in all of her strong points, and excels in any weakness that she may have.

The term *excels* does not mean that the boar should be excessive in a particular characteristic. For example, if your females are a little on the small side and you wish to increase wither size in your herd, the boar selected should have ideal size rather than being oversized. The oversized boar would increase the genetic variation for size in your herd, which is not what you are seeking to do.

THE MATING

The female hedgehog is polyestrus, which means that she is capable of having a number of litters within any one year. In the wild, she has two peak breeding periods, which coincide with the rainy season, longer daylight hours, warmer weather, and more readily available food items. Under captive conditions, these environmental factors are under breeder control, so hedgehogs can breed throughout the year.

It is customary, though by no means obligatory, for the sow to be taken to the boar's accommodations. This is because in his domain he is more self assertive, she less so than if she is on her home ground, where she may be more stubborn in allowing the mating to take place until she is quite ready. Normally, the sow is placed directly into her mate's pen, which should be cleared of its nestbox and other potential hiding places. Matters are then observed by the breeder just to be sure there are no undue problems.

The female is an induced ovulator, so if she is in estrus, the boar's presence is sufficient to prompt her to release eggs into the oviduct for fertilization by his sperm. If she is not ready to be bred, she will reject, in a forceful manner, all of his attempts and vocal beseechments to allow mating to occur. The boar is, however, a persistent creature and can unduly pester such a female. If it is obvious that she is becoming distressed, you should remove her and try again the next day.

If there is indeed an estrus cycle in the hedgehog, it is probably of very short duration, verging on spontaneous, so by the following day the sow should at least be more tolerant. Some breeders leave the sow with the male for two days, remove her for two days, and repeat the mating. They may even repeat this sequence again (Storer 1994), but this would seem to serve very little purpose. Providing there are no problems of compatibility, the Lermayers, at their Avalon Ranch Stud, leave the pair together for about seven days.

Studies in other pets show that repeat matings after a short rest period (24 hours) do serve to increase litter numbers; but, conversely, excessive matings may actually negatively affect the size of the litter. To what degree this is true or not in hedgehogs appears not to have been determined at this time, which is why the various methods mentioned are being tried out. Another approach to mating that is worthy of consideration if a given male is known to be very aggressive would be to place the sow in the male's pen, but with a wire partition between the two. Using this method, you can assess the sow's reaction without the need for the two to reach combat stations.

When the female is ready to be mated, she will drop her defenses and lower the spines on her back so that they lay flat. The male will then mount her and grasp some spines on her neck— much in the manner of cats when they mate. The actual copulation period is relatively short, two to three minutes, but may be repeated several times over any given period. Being crepuscular and nocturnal, the most favorable mating time will be the late evening. Once the mating period is over, the sow should be removed and placed back in her own accommodations.

GESTATION AND LITTER SIZE

The gestation period in the African pygmy hedgehog is about 35 days, give or take a day or two. Predicting the actual birth date is not always possible because you may not be sure when the eggs were actually fertilized. Mark it

herd, you may see an increase in the average litter size by one to three. However, the down side is that the larger the litter the greater the risks of postnatal deaths and youngsters lacking the substance of the smaller litter. With this in mind, you should not assume that larger litters are necessarily all good news in the development of a

A hedgehog breeding room. Note the spacious, well-appointed cages.

on your calendar or your pet's breeding-record card anyway, based on 35 days (five weeks) from the day you saw a mating, or assumed it may have taken place. The litter size is variable, depending on the combined effect of a number of influences. The known litter range is one to ten, with four to five being typical. With the establishment of a good

quality herd. What you should strive for is females that consistently produce litters of very healthy hoglets that have good birth weights. Additionally, hedghog mothers should be able to comfortably suckle without problems to their own health and vigor. But, the reverse extreme is no more desirable, so it comes down to the probability that a litter range of four to six may well be the optimum for quality and rearing potential. Breed for quality, not quantity. Because fertility and litter size do not have high heritable values, and are further greatly affected by environmental conditions, your philosophy must be that if you obtain a good mother who produces the required numbers, hang on to her!

THE PREGNANT SOW

If your sow, as she should be, is very familiar with being handled, you should make a point of regularly studying her underbelly. You will be aware of what her nipples look like and how much fat she carries. As she proceeds into the pregnancy, you will be aware of this because the nipples will slowly enlarge and "pink up." During the last ten days of the pregnancy, she will become noticeably plumper. By *careful* palpation, you may be able to feel the fetuses.

If you do not normally provide your pets with a nestbox, then one should be placed into the pen about 14 days prior to the estimated date of parturition. If the sow already has a nestbox that she uses as her sleeping quarters, so much the better, as she will more

likely use it than have births outside of a nestbox with which she may not be familiar. It must, of course, be large enough to accommodate her increased girth.

If your sow is of a somewhat nervous disposition, it is worthwhile placing the nestbox entrance toward the back of her pen. This will give her a greater feeling of security. If she is a very friendly and outgoing little girl, it may be placed sideways to the main pen entrance. This is the preferred situation, which even the apprehensive first timer may be confident with by the time of her third litter onwards. Also, you are better able to observe and assist when it is in this location.

It is said that the sow will move the box to the position she most likes, but my own observations suggest a simpler reason. Most breeders are using relatively small carry crates as breeding units and equip them with light plastic nestboxes. As the hedgehog moves around, it knocks the box into different positions, not deliberately. It is a foraging animal and will upturn such a box just to see what is underneath. Further, it will attempt to climb on top of a small nestbox, and may knock it over in the process. The answer is to secure the nestbox in some way.

The preferred temperature in the breeding room is in the range of 70-75°F (21-24°C). Some breeders prefer the upper range limit to be 3-4° higher, but excessive heat may stress the female and make her more likely to be cannibalistic. Be aware

During the pregnancy, the sow's food intake will steadily rise because she must nourish the growing fetuses. Be sure it is of good protein content. The addition of bread soaked in milk, or calcium powder sprinkled on the food, will be beneficial to ensure good bone growth and milk production. However, do not go overboard on either of these items, as an

A baby hedgehog several hours old. The gestation period for these animals is around 35 days, give or take a day or two.

that the temperature preference of one female may not be the same for another, so only by trial and error can you find the level most acceptable to all of your sows. The light cycle in the breeding room should be 12 hours on, 12 off. The use of a low-wattage blue light during the off period may prove beneficial in simulating moonlight conditions.

excess, especially of concentrated calcium powder, can be deleterious to her needs.

About six days prior to the expected day of birth, you should meticulously clean out the breeding pen. Place fresh woodshavings into the nestbox, but do not make the layer too deep. If she needs more, she will gather them herself from outside the nestbox. This will indicate that the births are imminent. Once the clean nestbox is in place, leave mom to her own devices. This situation should continue until at least 21 days after the birth.

Of course, she must be fed during this time, but do this so that there is as little disturbance as possible. Any fecal matter can be carefully removed using a long-handled spoon or scoop kept just for this purpose. A day before the anticipated births, you can reduce the sow's food intake so that her stomach is not full of food when parturition takes place. She will probably not want much food at this time anyway, not even on the day after the births.

PRIVACY AND THE BIRTHS

You will find that you have an almost overwhelming desire to inspect the nestbox on the due date of the babies' arrival. This will reach a dramatic peak when you hear the first little squeals that tell you that the world's finest litter of hedgehogs has just been born! Do *not* succumb to your desires, as this might just result in the shortest-lived litter of hoglets that your sow will ever produce.

Female hedgehogs are notoriously edgy just before, during, and after births. The slightest disturbance may cause them to devour entire litters. This is a protective instinct—they would rather kill the babies than let a predator make a meal of them. You may be perceived as that predator until the sow learns from experience that you represent no threat at this time. Even a very friendly female can change in her nature when breeding. Likewise, the maiden female may become both frightened or confused at the time of her first litter. She may abandon the babies, or mistake one or more of them for the afterbirth and consume them.

Should this happen, it is probable that things will be better on the occasion of her second litter. If not, this suggests that she is a very nervous individual and has no further use as a breeder. Alternatively, there may be something wrong in her environment—noise, disturbance, other pets too close for her comfort, incorrect housing, lighting or heating, inadequate nutrition, or the like—and things will not improve until you find out what the problem is.

Experienced breeders may be able to inspect youngsters within the first week of their birth, but it is stressed that the novice breeder should not attempt this, or do so at his own peril.

REARING

When the babies are born, they have a thin membrane covering the small spines. This shrivels up within a few hours, and the spines grow rapidly. At first, they are white, but

each passing week. By about the third day, if she is attending them with care, she should prove to be a good mother. If any of the babies should scramble out of their nestbox at this time, and in the following days, they should be gathered up on a plastic spoon or similar object and carefully placed back into

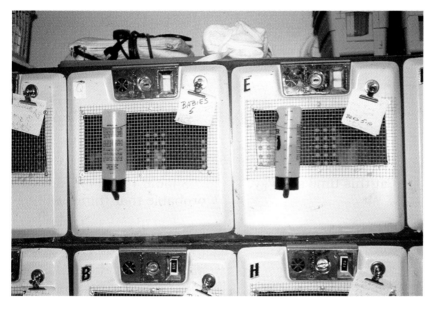

Careful records to monitor due dates are essential to successful breeding.

this gives way to brown or black as the spines get longer (assuming the coloration is of the normal wild type). Now that the babies are born, the appetite of the mother returns with a vengeance. She will need anything from four to eight times her normal rations as the hoglets grow—depending on the size of the litter. The chances of her being cannibalistic recede with

the nestbox. Do not handle them at this time, as it may prompt the sow to kill them.

Once they are about three weeks or older, you may carefully handle them in order to establish sexes. The whole business of handling the babies from a young age is very much a matter of trial and error until you know how each female reacts. This is why it is best to be cautious

A newborn litter snug and secure in its nestbox.

with a newly acquired female, or first-time mother. When you know that the mother tolerates you with her newborns, you can then start weighing, marking, and carefully inspecting youngsters. But until then proceed very carefully.

The weaning process will begin when the hoglets are three or more weeks of age. How long it will take will be influenced by the nature of the mother and the size of the litter. Normally, the babies will be independent of their mother by four to six weeks of age. By now you should have been handling the youngsters on a daily basis in order to socialize them as much as possible. Never allow your herd size to grow beyond your ability to devote sufficient time to the babies during this vital period of their lives.

FOSTERING

If you have two or more sows, it is beneficial to try and mate them at the same time so that their litters are born within a day or so of each other. This makes the whole operation rather easier and smoother to manage. It also means that if a mother rejects her offspring, or has an especially large litter, you can try and foster the youngsters under another sow. This is always a delicate and chancy operation, but it is better than losing any of the litter.

If fostering is attempted, it should be done while the youngsters are under four days of age. Otherwise, rejection is more likely. Transfer the babies on a spoon so that you minimize the risk of your scent being on them. In other pets, fostering is often completed by smearing some of the mother's litter on the youngsters to mask the fostered baby's scent. Actually, I am not sure this is of any importance. Mothers are far more able than we give them credit for in knowing which babies are theirs, regardless of how we try to mask the baby's scent. What is of far more importance is just how strong her mothering instincts are. If they are high, she will readily accept new babies; if they are not, she will soon kill them. A good foster mother in any species is a very valuable addition to a breeding herd. If you get one, be sure to retain it.

A final comment on fostering is that it should not be done simply to ensure that the offspring of a bad mother can be reared and then sold. This is a dangerous policy that merely spreads the genes for poor motherhood into the population as a whole. In Gouldian finches, for example, it has resulted in the fact that the majority of chicks are fostered to Bengalese finches because the incidence of poor parental hens is so high in the domestic species. We do not need to move in that direction.

will soon lose breeding condition. This will be reflected in less vigorous babies of progressively poor quality. The sow will become run down. Her effective breeding life, indeed lifespan, will probably be reduced. Three to four litters a year is ample, more than this is

This hoglet is being fed a milk supplement by means of an eye dropper. Handrearing any baby animal requires great care and patience.

HOW MANY LITTERS PER YEAR?

The number of times that you breed your females each year is, of course, a subjective matter. There are those (cash crazy) who want as many litters as possible, so they keep their sows continually in a pregnant state. This is a very short-sighted policy that has little long-term merit for either the hobby as a whole, or the individual's breeding program. A hard-bred sow

pure greed. After each litter is weaned, you should rest the sow for about a month. Ideally, place her in large accommodations where she can exercise and generally restore the condition that was depleted by the very severe strain that is always attendant with the birth and nursing process.

COLOR BREEDING

The colors in any animal species are of two distinct types. There are those that are within the natural range of variation in the species, and there are those resulting from mutation and recombination of mutations. Sometimes it can be difficult to distinguish one from the other, as with creams that may be the result of mutation, or be the lightest extreme of the natural color range. Likewise, a very dark brown or black may be a heavily pigmented individual of extreme natural type; or it may be the result of a mutation, either dominant or recessive, that has actually changed the basic genotype of the individual. At this time the following colors are reported:

ALBINO: This would be a mutational color. If the hedgehog coat is regarded as being agouti, the albino genotype would be *aa,* meaning non-agouti. The mutation is recessive in mode of inheritance.

SNOWFLAKE: This is all white but with a black mask and dark eye color.

WHITE, DARK-EYED: This may be the same as the snowflake and may be termed dark-eyed or ruby-eyed.

CREAM: This is actually a light tan to reddish color.

POLKA DOT: This has a mottled or striped appearance.

NORMAL: This is the wild-type coloration, which in the mouse, rabbit, guinea pig, and many other mammals with a similar hair-band coloration, is known as agouti—for the South American rodent of that name and color pattern.

The genetic base of these colors has not yet been established. Once it is known, it will open up tremendous possibilities if these colors are, in fact, mutations and not just natural varieties created by what are known as gene modifiers. It would not be unreasonable to expect red, blue, piebald, roan, and even tortoiseshell, as well as patterned varieties of various designs as are seen in other pets.

However, sometimes a reported color mutation in an individual is the result of environmental conditions, not a mutation. For example, a dietary deficiency or an illness early in a youngster's life can result in abnormal functioning of melanin in the cells of the coat. Such a color would not be transmitted to that individual's offspring. The problem may have derived prenatally, so that the offspring was born a non-normal color, thus giving the appearance of being mutational. Be these things as they may, there is much to look forward to in the coming years where color breeding is concerned.

Breeding Strategy

The limitations of a single chapter on breeding strategy and theory mean that only a few aspects can be discussed at primer level. Nonetheless, it is hoped that it will prompt you to further study, and at the least provide food for thought. The small size, cuteness, and, it must be said, the thought that quick profits can be made from these pets, will bring into the hobby a number of people who have little or no understanding of breeding, and even less of its theory.

Even those that have practical experience on the subject may have little knowledge of the effect of genes on animals. This is quite obvious from statements one hears in most pet pursuits. Let us consider a few miscellaneous matters that will be of significance very quickly in these pets.

RECORD KEEPING

Since hedgehogs are so new on the pet scene, it is crucial that breeders keep detailed records of all of their matings and litters. Your memory is extremely fallible, a fact that has been proven many times when related to animal breeding. In order to keep records, you must first have a sound system of individual hedgehog identification. Your permanent options are ear tagging, closed leg banding

Handrearing. Though it is young, this hoglet already has well-developed teeth, which you can see if you look closely.

(rings), microchip implanting, and tattooing. At this time, none of these methods have gained general acceptance, so the recommended method has yet to be resolved. Temporary identification can be by means of split leg bands, which can be color coded (single or double colors) and numbered, or by using paint. It is rump (either left, right, or center), you can easily devise an identification system that should cope with all of your likely practical needs.

Next, you need your record cards. Your system can be as simple or as complex as is felt suited to your objectives, which themselves can be limited or broad based. You

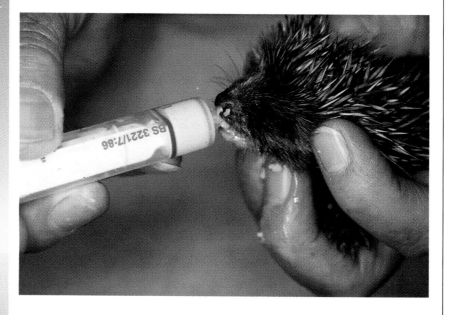

This hedge-hoglet is being hand-fed. This procedure is necessary when a hedgehog litter is orphaned, unless the youngsters can be fostered to another sow. Photo by Michael Gilroy.

advisable that you use a non-toxic water-based poster paint that can readily be removed if so desired. This is presently the most popular method. You can use green, blue, or red—brown, black, and yellow are less desirable colors on the normal-colored hedgehog. By placing a color on the head, shoulder, mid level, or should, however, include the following:

1. Individual records. Each breeding male and female should have its own card, which should document basic data such as the sex, age, color, and sire/dam of the individual. It is certainly useful if you can include a good photograph of the individual and keep it with

the record card. Alternatively, use a drawing to show any pattern markings that may differ from the normal color pattern of the hedgehog.

This card should record all matings of the individual, numbers of offspring, and the number of them that survived to the age when they went to new homes. It should note

any youngster dies, this will be recorded, as will the reason for the death—if it can be established. Likewise, any problems will be noted along with the treatment given.

If any youngsters are born with abnormalities that are such that you cull them, you should still make notes on the abnormality. Do not just

Closeup of a breeding cage used by a professional hedgehog breeder.

illness and any other information that may prove useful in the future.

2. Breeding records. These cards will record the results of matings. They will indicate which male and female were paired and on what date. When the litter is born, you will note the gestation period, the number of offspring, their sexes, and their colors. If

destroy them and pretend they never happened. This does nothing for the hobby as a whole, nor, indeed, your own program. Further, do not "hide" negative results. If everyone takes the same approach, then everyone loses out on information that might be to the mutual benefit of all breeders.

BREEDING OBJECTIVES

At this time, breeders are in the enviable position of being able to base their programs almost entirely on measurable objectives rather than on aesthetics. This means that if you wish to produce pets within a given size and weight range, you can compare your offspring and select breeding stock based on your results. If height is an objective, it is easy to see if your program is achieving its objective or not.

The minute you breed for beauty, you are in a subjective situation. This means that your own view of what is desirable may not be in keeping with the mainstream thoughts of others. In other words, assessment of what is good and bad no longer becomes measurable per se, but is determined by opinion rather than by facts.

Presently, it is very important that you set your objectives on breeding very healthy stock. If a given boar or sow shows, via its offspring, that it is producing hoglets of poor health in any way, it should not be used for further breeding.

Good temperament is another very high priority in this pet. The problem is that it can be very difficult to say whether poor temperament in a given individual (or litter) is a result of its breeding or its environment—specifically the way it has been handled (or not) from a young age. This being so, you can reduce the possibility of the breeding (genetic) influence by not getting involved in close inbreeding. Given the limited gene pool from which the present pets have been derived, it is true to say that all of them are probably inbred to a greater or lesser degree.

It is thus a case of minimizing further instances of this until there is some data base that might give us more information on the genetic state of this pet, and of any known linkages between desirable and undesirable features and traits. There is evidence in other animals to support the view that close inbreeding, such as mother/son, father/daughter, and sibling matings, will result in undesirable temperaments. Conversely, there is also evidence in rats and guinea pigs that after as many as 25 generations of very close inbreeding (brother/sister), the resulting population was both more vigorous and more disease resistant than the original stocks. However, in the early generations, there were many instances of

The practice of self-anointing is instinctive at a very early age. This two-week-old hedgehog is anointing even before its eyes have opened.

inbreeding depression and abnormalities. Some lines even failed to survive.

The fact that few breeders will actually cull out animals with poor temperament means that the positive effect of selection will not be working to minimize the negative aspect of this trait. Further, no breeding is ever likely to be able to maintain the sort of stock numbers that are utilized in the institute experiments just quoted. Caution, therefore, dictates that breeding should be restricted to distant, rather than close, relatives.

Most breeders, like the customers they supply, will probably have a preference for one or more color patterns. Your policy on color should be that breeding for it must be done only if there is no evidence along the way that health and temperament are being sacrificed. There is some genetic support for the view that color paling may by linked to the degeneration of other traits, but there is little scientifically analyzed data to say one way or the other if this is so in hedgehogs.

Clearly, the more objectives you set, the harder it will be to achieve success across *all* of them. As you make progress in one characteristic, it may be that you will lose ground in another. What you must do is to try and avoid making selections based on what are actually trivial features when compared to the priorities that you had set initially. But this does not mean that your priorities, other than for health and breeding vigor, will not change as your program progresses. Once you are satisfied that you have achieved a high-priority objective, it becomes a case of trying to maintain the standard that you have achieved for it, while giving higher priority to another feature that is in need of improvement.

BREEDING SYSTEMS

Over the years, there have been very many systems put forward that are believed to create better individuals in a given population if they are applied. Most of them are based on sound genetic principles. But in each case, they rely heavily on the breeder's ability to make sound judgments on the animals selected for onward breeding. Without sound judgment, no breeding system will prove to be effective. The following are but a few systems that can be utilized by the average breeder.

One is known as the independent culling-level method. Most practical breeders utilize this system, even if they do not recognize its formal name. What you do is list the qualities you are seeking in your pets and grade them excellent, good, average, or low. You then decide on the standard you will accept. You might reject any animal that does not score at least average on every feature. The system works well enough in that it should ensure that the overall standard of your stock improves at each generation. At each of them, you can adjust the qualifying limit.

The drawback of the independent culling-level method is that it implies that all features selected have equal merit, which is rarely the case. Further, you may discard an individual that was graded poorly in one or two features, but was quite outstanding in others. The culling-level method is superior to the tandem method, in which you concentrate on one feature at a time. This can produce spectacular results in a short space of time, but it can take a long time to work through all of the features. Further, as one does, so the standard of features previously raised may degenerate considerably.

Independent culling can be improved by placing the desired characteristics in a list in which each character is given a score based on its importance. Health would rank 10, temperament 8, color 6, size 4, weight 3, and so on. The preceding figures given are merely examples of the method, not how you might actually evaluate qualities, though the first two named should always rank above all else. Using this method, you then decide what *total* score you will accept in a potential breeding individual.

Using this method, you are better able to list far more features than under independent culling in which, by so doing, you

system somewhat by marking all features out of, say, 10 points and then applying a coefficient in order to take into account the value of that feature. This is superior because it is easier to score against a consistent number (out of 10 in this case) than against a declining number, as in the 10, 8, 6, and so on method. The coefficient must be

A male and female settling into their travel cage. The bi-level arrangement provides comfort for the animals and prevents unplanned pregnancies.

would raise the possibility of discarding useful individuals simply because they fell below the set level in one or two of these features. The drawback to a total score utilizing many features is that you may have to start with some very high scores for prime features in order to accommodate some score for less important features.

You can streamline the

considered very carefully; it must not tilt the system to the point that it does not allow a generally good animal from being discarded simply because it did not score so well on a prime feature. This said, the objective is to favor individuals that excel in the features you are in need of improving.

If health is the priority, it might have a coefficient of

5, temperament 4, color 3, size 3, weight 2, length 2, and so on. If an individual scored 7 out of 10 for health, then 7 would be multiplied by 5 to give 35 points for that feature. If it scored 6 for color, this would be multiplied by 3 to give 18, and so on. Once again, you determine what the qualifying score is for retention of individuals. It is obvious that you must be able to judge each

the risk of selling one that matures to be better than its apparent worth a month or two earlier. But this is bound to happen anyway because not every hoglet will mature at the same rate. You are invariably limited by space, time, or finances in how many youngsters you can retain.

As the system gets underway and results are forthcoming in subsequent generations, you can alter

Hedgehog litters vary in size. Litters have been known to range from one to ten, with four to five being typical.

individual consistently.

One way to help in this direction is to assess each individual more than once over a given time period. This has the advantage of enabling you to see how that individual has improved, or not, as it matured. Of course, it does mean that you may have to retain a number of individuals longer than usual in order to overcome

and fine tune the coefficient to take success, failure, and new priorities into account. What you must do with any breeding system is to stay with it until you are quite sure it is either succeeding, or failing, your needs. Very often, breeders will drop or change systems before they have been given a fair chance to prove themselves.

HERITABILITY AND LINKAGE

One of the problems that any breeder faces is that all characteristics are not inherited in the same way. For example, color is basically quite simple in its mode of inheritance and can invariably be written by means of a formula. An albino hedgehog mated to another albino will produce only albino offspring. An albino paired the calculations become. You have to take into account their interactions. Other characteristics (in fact, most others), such as temperament, litter size, wither height, snout length, resistance to disease, fertility, and so on, are controlled by many genes—they are said to be polygenic traits. Manipulating them is not so easy and is made that much more difficult

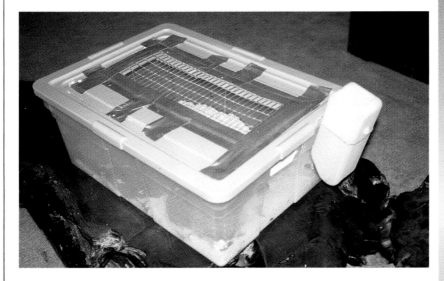

Weaning pens should be thoroughly cleaned before they house each new litter.

to any other colored hedgehog will produce no albinos, but every single youngster in the litter will carry the albino gene. This is because the genes that control colors are major genes in their action. They are readily apparent and can easily be manipulated by you, the breeder. Of course, the more color mutations you are dealing with, the more complex because some have low heritable values, others have high values, and there is a gradation between the two extremes.

For example, if you were trying to produce a line of females with high litter numbers, this would probably prove to be a difficult task. Litter size is controlled by what are termed non-additive polygenes. Manipulating them is very complex. Conversely, conformational characteristics are probably additive in their mode of inheritance. This means that if you breed tall males and females, you will normally move the average height of the stock upward. Of course, the reverse is true if small parents are used at each generation. Nervousness has a quite high heritable value, which means you can rapidly reduce its incidence by careful selection of parental stock.

MISCONCEPTIONS ABOUT BREEDING

There are a few misconceptions that are often heard in pet-breeding circles, and are already being passed around in the hedgehog hobby. You are always advised to question anything that you are told or read in respect to breeding, indeed, all aspects of your pets—from housing to feeding to health care. By so doing, you will build up a balanced knowledge that has been gathered across a wide range of sources.

One misconception is that albino animals are usually inferior in one or more ways. This is not so. Most quality ferrets are, in fact, albinos, as are many mice and rats. There are albino rabbits, guinea pigs, fish, and birds—all of excellent quality. There are albino dogs and cats; but because they are not generally fashionable, they are usually culled or discarded. One of the problems is that people often confuse albinism with the color white. In some white animals, problems may indeed be linked to their color. An albino has no color pigmentation—the red you see in its eyes is the hemoglobin of the blood. A white has pigment; this may be seen only as a ruby color in the eyes or some pigment on the nails and nose. At this time, there is no way of saying whether albino hedgehogs, as they are bred, will be popular or not.

Another misconception is that certain colors are linked to nervousness. In general, this is not so, at least in any of the present pet species. Color is normally inherited quite independently of other characteristics. What might be more true to say is that a given color may be associated—not truly linked—with nervousness, poor health, and so on. The difference may seem subtle, or a play on words, but it is important.

When a color mutation appears, it does not

necessarily do so in a superb individual. For example, an animal with a beautiful color mutation may have a very nervous disposition, and you have read that nervousness has a quite high heritable value. Further, even a sound-looking individual may be carrying any number of recessive abnormal genes in its makeup (genotype). Now,

color becomes associated with the problems. Linkage is a quite different situation. Here, there is a real genetic link between certain genes. If this linkage is to desirable qualities, then it is to the good; but sometimes the desired qualities are linked to undesirable ones. In the former instance (association), it is possible to separate the

A hedgehog mom and her youngsters enjoying a meal. Considering their small size, hedgehogs are very hearty eaters.

in order to maximize on the color mutation, breeders will often inbreed to fix the color in their stock.

As they do, they will, of course, intensify any other weakness, such as nervousness. Further, they greatly increase the possibility of bringing unwanted recessive genes to the surface, and so the

unwanted characteristics from the color. But in the latter instance, this is much more difficult, and not so readily under direct breeder control.

The final matter that I will comment on is the statement that inbreeding creates abnormalities and problems. If two animals have no given abnormalities in their genotype, then no amount of inbreeding will create abnormalities. But if, hidden in the complexity of polygenic characteristics, there is a recessive gene that could result in a problem if the genetic background was such as to favor the increase of these unwanted genes, then inbreeding dramatically raises the potential to create such a background. Further, it cannot be assumed that all characteristics are best in a pure-breeding (homozygous) state, which is the direction inbreeding will take them.

The ramifications of these facts not only bring to the surface abnormal features but also trigger what is known as inbreeding depression, where a number of characteristics are affected.

So that you have a concept of what inbreeding actually means, it is best defined as the breeding of individuals that are more closely related than the average of the population from which they were derived. The most popular breeding method used in most animals is called linebreeding; but be aware that it is still inbreeding at a less-intense level, so its potential problems (and virtues) are diluted.

The reason why close inbreeding (father/daughter, mother/son, brother/sister, and similar other matings) is not recommended at this stage in the development of the hedgehog as a pet is because it will no doubt bring to the surface any problems hidden in the genetic makeup of the present limited hedgehog lines. This could badly damage the reputation of this pet. At the best of times, inbreeding is an excellent tool in the hands of those who know what they are doing; but it can be disastrous when practiced without knowledge of its implications, and without very rigid selection and culling.

When they are old enough, orphaned youngsters can be fed baby food. Eventually, they can be switched over to more substantial foods, including canned dog food.

Health Care

Hedgehogs are very hardy little animals, but, like any other creature, they can fall victim to a large number of diseases and conditions. Because they are such new pets, little research has been applied to any diseases to which they are especially prone, and no vaccinations are specifically produced for them. If you have any particular concerns about your hedgehog's health, check with your vet.

The main thrust of the health care that you provide for your hedgehog must be in prevention rather than in cure, so this is what we will consider in this chapter.

GENERAL HYGIENE

Although it is a well-known fact, the reality is that very many diseases in pets arise due to no other reason than poor hygiene, often coupled with inadequate diet and stress-causing conditions. Let us go through each of the likely areas where owners are often lax in hygiene, and which increase the likelihood of pathogenic colonization.

Food and Water Containers

These items should be cleaned daily, not every few days, or whenever the dishes look rather disgusting! Any that become cracked or chipped should be discarded and replaced. If you keep two or more hedgehogs for breeding, and they are in separate accommodations, be sure to place dishes back in the same enclosure from which they came.

Health Tips About Food

All foods should be stored in cool dark cupboards where there is no risk of mice or other rodents contaminating them with fecal matter. Never feed any food if you are unsure of its freshness. If it smells "off," throw it away. Always remove

Good husbandry, such as regular bedding changes, will go a long way in keeping your hedgehog healthy.

Your pet's food bowls should be in good condition. Discard any that become chipped or cracked. Photo courtesy Rolf C. Hagen Corp.

uneaten food items within a matter of hours, especially those such as moist mashes, vegetables, meats, and the like, which quickly sour and attract flies. Dry biscuit/chow foods can be left down for longer periods.

Physical Examinations

Make a point of inspecting your hedgehog each day, and certainly each week at the latest. Minor cuts and abrasions quickly heal; but if left unattended, they can be the site for secondary infection by parasites and other pathogens, which are able to gain easy access through them to the bloodstream. Wash all cuts with a very mild saline solution and then apply an antiseptic lotion or gel to the wound to protect it while it heals. Bad wounds must, of course, be treated by your vet.

Lumps or other swellings should be referred to your vet—they may be insect stings, snake bites, tumors, or simply bruises. Whatever they are, they need professional inspection and treatment. Lice, fleas, and ticks can be a problem to hedgehogs in the wild, due to their low-to-the-ground foraging habits. They should be no more a problem to them under captive conditions than they are to your dog and cat. Look carefully around their ears, muzzle, and underparts. Any that are seen can easily be eradicated with modern treatments from your vet, who will advise you on how to apply them.

Cleaning Your Hedgehog's Housing

Your hedgehog's home, be it indoors or outdoors, should be thoroughly cleaned each week. Its nest box, in particular, must be maintained in an immaculate condition. If lice, mites, or ticks have been a problem, all bedding material must be removed and burned. Do not simply dump it in a pile in your yard. This merely creates a breeding ground for these pests and other bacteria and fungi.

Likewise, do not keep rotting piles of vegetation anywhere near a hedgehog enclosure, as they, too, are ideal sites for pathogenic colonization. Floor covering material should be replaced on a regular basis. Soiled floor covering should be disposed of properly—in a bin or other container away from your pet's accommodations.

Personal Cleanliness

Always wash your hands before and after handling your hedgehog. Remember, you can be the means by which bacteria are transported from one animal or place to your pet. Be especially thorough in matters of personal cleanliness if you have been anywhere near lots of animals, or if you have been near one that you know is ill or recovering from an illness—the more so if it is a friend's hedgehog.

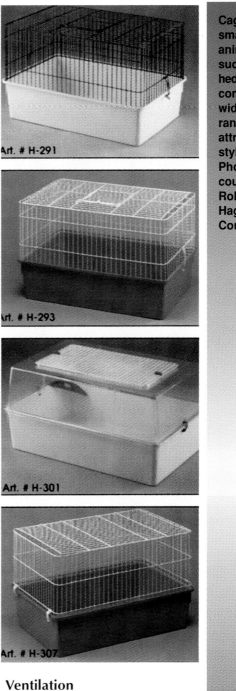

Art. # H-291

Art. # H-293

Art. # H-301

Art. # H-307

Cages for small animals such as hedgehogs come in a wide range of attractive styles. Photo courtesy Rolf C. Hagen Corp.

Ventilation

If you keep your hedgehog in an outbuilding, and the more so if other pets share this unit, be sure it is well ventilated, especially during

Right:
Corn cobs
are a good
absorbent
lining for
cages with
removable
trays.
Photo
courtesy
Rolf C.
Hagen
Corp. *Far
right:* This
hedgehog
seems
eager to
be let go
to explore
on its own.
If you do
give your
pet free
access to
any area
of your
home,
make sure
that all
safety
hazards
have been
eliminated.

the warm periods. Lack of ventilation is a prime cause of pathogenic build-up in such buildings, and thus it is a major cause of the spread of disease. Avoid using hay and straw as bedding material because they can be the source of fungal infections via the spores that can survive in them for long periods.

Remember, for your pet to become diseased, or even ill, bacteria must first get to it, then in it, and then multiply. You cannot build an impenetrable defense around your pet, but there is no need to provide an ideal breeding ground for these unwanted organisms. If you diligently apply consistent efforts to the areas discussed, you will dramatically reduce the risk of disease befalling your pet.

QUARANTINE

If you decide to become a hedgehog breeder, or even to acquire a small collection of these pets, you are advised to have some indoor facility where newly acquired individuals can be kept isolated from the rest of your stock. This is a wise precaution because it gives time for any incubating illnesses to show themselves. During the quarantine period, which should be at least 14 days and up to 30 days, you can routinely treat the new addition for external and internal parasites. You can also more easily monitor its feeding habits and steadily adjust its diet to that which you have selected.

KNOW WHEN YOUR HEDGEHOG IS UNWELL

The following are all signs of ill health: Weeping eyes, runny nose, foul-smelling ears, swellings, abrasions, cuts, wheezy breathing, repeated vomiting, diarrhea (the more so if it is blood

Pet shops stock a variety of fine bedding materials. Photo courtesy Rolf C. Hagen Corp.

streaked), constipation, repeated coughing or choking (especially so if blood is brought up), loss of hair or spines, and any bald spots on the body, especially if they display a flaked appearance or have whorls on them.

In many instances, the first signs of a problem may not be physical, but rather in behavioral changes from what is normal. To appreciate these changes, you must, of course, know what is normal for your particular hedgehog. Has it suddenly started to show disinterest in its food when it is normally a ravenous eater? Is it refusing known items that are normally much relished? Is it hiding away when normally it would be out and about? Does it seem perturbed or in pain when you handle it? Does it seem to be scratching excessively, or trying to bite at something in its fur?

To know these things, you must watch its day-to-day habits, including the way it eats and which items are preferred. Note the day and time of any behavioral changes. This may be useful data to your vet if the hedgehog starts to show physical signs of ill health some days later. Likewise, note the progression of any physical signs of ill health. A runny nose might not prompt you to call the vet; but if a day later your pet's eyes show signs of discharge, this may be part of the disease's pathogenesis (mode of development).

ACT PROMPTLY

Once you have decided that your pet is ill, the sooner some form of action is taken the better. Ideally, you will contact your vet and relate the physical and behavioral signs. Do not wait for another day or so to see how things go. This merely allows the problem to reach a more advanced stage, thus making treatment more prolonged and costly. If the clinical signs that are bothering you are limited to your hedgehog's fecal matter being loose, you should withhold the moist food items for 24 hours and supply only hard chow and comparable items. The condition should clear up. If it persists and gets worse, contact your vet. Likewise, your pet can catch a chill, and the result

Always wash your hands before and after handling your hedgehog.

may be runny eyes and a small nasal discharge of clear liquid. In this case, restrict the hedgehog to a warm room (a few degrees higher than its normal living conditions). The problem should rectify itself within 24 to 36 hours. But if it deteriorates at all, do call your vet.

You can obtain commercial hospital cages, which come in a variety of styles. Alternatively, you can use a dull-emitter infrared lamp suspended over, or in front of, a cage used for ill animals. Place the lamp at one end of the cage so that if your pet gets too hot, it can move to a more comfortable heat level. The cage should be fitted with a thermometer, and it is preferable that the lamp is wired through a thermostat so the temperature can be

maintained at a constant level. In an emergency, you can use a regular tungsten light bulb as a heat source, but be sure your hedgehog has a nestbox so that it can retreat from the glare of such a lamp.

THE STRESS FACTOR
The subject of stress is receiving more and more attention by researchers, veterinarians, and those who keep and breed animals. Its main problem is that a stressor (something that causes stress) in one individual may not be so in another. Its effect on any animal can be considerable, so you should understand the basics of what it is all about—it is also becoming a major problem to humans as well as pets and other animals. Unlike fear, which is a condition

elicited as a direct response to a real danger or threat, stress is a subconscious response to something that may be missing, or to something that is quite abnormal to the species or individual. For example, a highly social species can become badly stressed if it is denied the company of its own kind, or, at the least, company of another animal with which it can form a relationship. Conversely, a species, such as most hedgehogs, could become stressed simply by being made to coexist with its own kind in close proximity. This is because hedgehogs, in the main, are solitary creatures by nature.

However, even within species that are highly social, there is a required area, small though it may be, that each individual must have around it. If this area is reduced, then there comes a point where overcrowding is the result: this creates stress. It works in reverse for hedgehogs. If each individual has a given area of space to itself, then the presence of another conspecific may not induce stress. The problem is that we do not know how much space each hedgehog needs to be in a relaxed state.

Although stressors cannot, at least with our present knowledge, be placed in a hierarchal index, it has been reasonably established that the more natural a behavior pattern is, the greater the possibility it will result in stress if the animal is denied the opportunity to express that pattern. For example, a hedgehog is a foraging animal. If it is restrained in

Sanitary conditions are necessary for all hedgehogs, but especially so for those that are bred.

a small cage where it cannot forage, it will become stressed. Boredom is another stressor of great importance, which is why you should try to make your pet's accommodations and its lifestyle as interesting and natural as possible.

Excessive handling, interference when feeding or resting, overcrowding, and being moved to new environments are other obvious stressors that affect all animals, including your pet hedgehog. Certain noises, and excessive and continual lighting, are likely to be high stressors for an animal such as a hedgehog, which is basically nocturnal and active in darker lighting at a time when noise is normally at a low level.

The effect of stress may show itself in numerous ways. The pet may lick or bite at its fur to the degree that not only is it denuded of hair but also creates wounds that might fester. It may practice copro-, ligno-, geo-, or hyperphagia. These terms refer to the eating of fecal matter, wood, or soil, or simply overeating. It may drink excessively. Breeding willingness and ability may be reduced or absent. Parental anomalies such as cannibalism, not uncommon in some hedgehog species, or abandonment of young, may become apparent. A pet may show signs of aggression to its owner, or it may start to go off its food. These are but a few of the ways stress can manifest itself.

Of course, many of these conditions might have an alternate source. This merely compounds the

Shown here are the few tools needed for basic hedgehog care.

The hedgehog is primarily a solitary animal, and chance encounters in the wild last only long enough for breeding. The male is often smaller than the female.

problem of identifying this condition. Your pet could bite at itself excessively because it has fleas or lice. It may drink excessively because it has a kidney or other disorder. It may eat its young because it is being underfed and knows it cannot rear a litter of babies—or there may be something in the environment that is perturbing the mother. However, if living conditions and nutrition are satisfactory, you must consider stress as a health factor and conduct your own investigation to see what might be causing it.

When a pet is stressed, this reduces the performance of its immune system, so it is much more open to pathogenic attack than normal. All of these reactions are compensatory: they are ways in which the individual is subconsciously trying to adapt to the situation it finds itself in—much as you might find yourself twisting a button on your coat, or doing likewise to a wedding ring or necklace, or some other comparable habit developed from stress or subconscious nervousness.

If you try to avoid any of the situations discussed, you minimize the risk of stress in your pet. Bear in mind that the moment you purchase your hedgehog and take it home will be the first stressful situation, so make things as pleasant, quiet, and relaxing as possible while it settles in.

INTERNAL PARASITES

The fossorial (adapted for digging) mode of hedgehog food consumption is such that hedgehogs are more

This hedgehog is having its nails clipped. In the wild, the nails would naturally wear down. Pet hedgehogs require regular nail clipping.

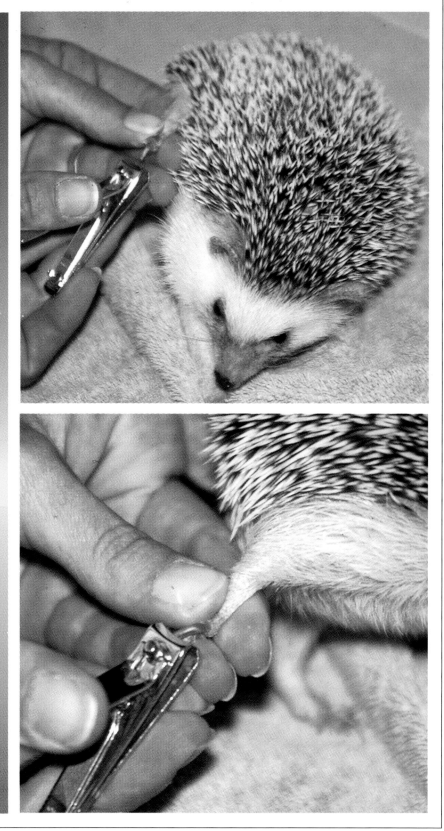

A tractable hedgehog that is used to its owner will probably not object to having its nails clipped.

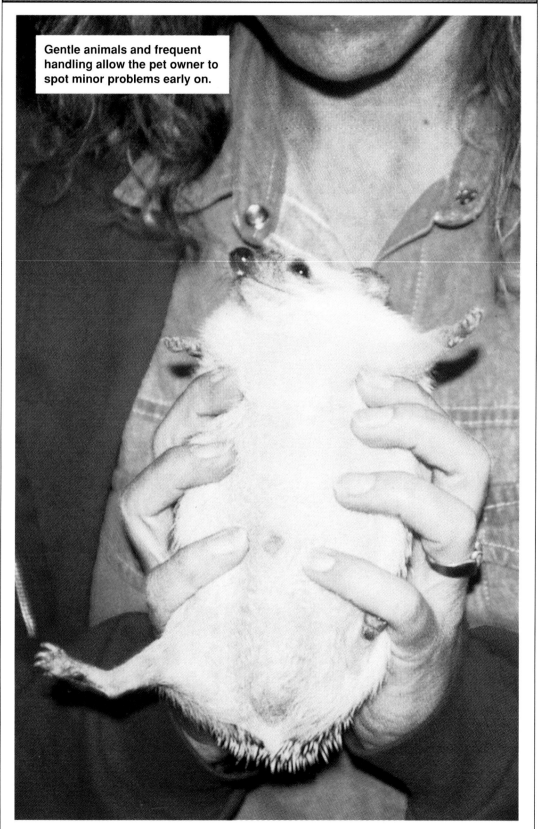

Gentle animals and frequent handling allow the pet owner to spot minor problems early on.

prone than some other pets to inhaling or ingesting the eggs of internal parasitic worms. These worms may be either roundworms or tapeworms—much as are found in dogs, cats, and other animals. If your hedgehog is kept in an outdoor enclosure, and especially if the enclosure contains an area of soil, you should routinely worm your pet about every two to three months. Your vet can do an egg count on your pet's fecal matter if you wish to ascertain if it has a higher-than-tolerable amount of worms within its digestive tract.

Worms are present in the digestive system of all animals and normally do not present a problem. It is when they reach infestation levels that ill health follows. This is because they deny the host the benefit of the food that it is eating. Its abdomen swells, and eventually it may lose interest in feeding; or it may start to vomit shortly after it has eaten. You should know the approximate weight of your pet so that appropriate dosages of medicines can be administered.

POSTMORTEM

In the event that your pet should die without having displayed any outward signs of a health problem, I would urge you to arrange for your vet to conduct a postmortem on the hedgehog. This is especially important if you are to replace the pet, or are attempting to develop a small breeding herd. Although postmortems do not always reveal the cause of death, they very often can.

Such knowledge may enable you to adopt a husbandry strategy that will reduce the risk of the same thing happening again. At the same time, there is a present need to gather as much information as possible about hedgehog ailments, diseases, and treatments under captive conditions. This may prove very useful to other owners and breeders.

HOME DIAGNOSIS AND TREATMENTS

The cost of veterinary treatments does not get any cheaper with the passage of time. However, against this you must balance the value of your pet, not just in regard to its material cost, but in the enjoyment that it provides for you and your family. Avoid all temptations to self

diagnose and treat your little pet. The problem is that serious diseases cannot readily be identified purely by clinical means.

Blood tests and fecal microscopy are invariably obligatory. Unless a correct diagnosis has been made, it is impossible to apply a treatment without taking a very high risk that it will be useless. It may even worsen the situation. Sometimes medicines can be used concurrently with each other; at other times, they may double up on a common constituent that could prove toxic. Unless you have pharmaceutical or veterinary training, you cannot know their effects.

If you concentrate your efforts into preventive husbandry techniques, as discussed in this chapter, your little hedgehog has every chance of living a happy and healthy life.

Hedgehogs are relatively hardy and long-lived pets that require a minimum in the way of health care.

In captivity, a hedgehog must be provided with a diet that is varied enough to ensure balanced nutrition.

The Hedgehog Species

In this chapter, the numerous hedgehog species, including the spiny tenrecs, are described. Their general lifestyle is not included as this is much the same for all members. Here we are more concerned with specific details of appearance, breeding data, (as far as it has been established), and other factual aspects of the individual species. Before discussing the species, and for those not familiar with the way animals are classified and named, a very brief explanation of the subject might prove useful and interesting to would-be enthusiasts of these (or any other) animal species.

CLASSIFICATION PRIMER

In order that any single animal, or group of them, can be referred to rapidly and without the risk of being confused with other similar-looking animals, a system of identification is essential, especially when there are over 1,000,000 known animals on our planet (and many more yet to be discovered). Such a system was developed in the 18th century by a Swedish naturalist named Carolus Linnaeus. It is called the Binomial System of Nomenclature.

Unlike identification keys, which use artificial similarities in order to divide animals into groups—such as those with wings, those that live in water, and so on—the Binomial System of Nomenclature is based on believed evolutionary affinities between animals, and groups of them. A whale lives in water, but it is not a fish because it has lungs and breaths air. It also develops its offspring in a placenta, feeds its babies via mammae, and has hair. Each of these features tells us that it is a mammal, just like a dog, cat, or human, but one that has evolved to live in an aquatic environment.

All mammals are placed in the class Mammalia, which is but one of many classes. Birds, all of whom have feathers, lay eggs, and have scales on their legs, are grouped in the class called Aves. Snakes and lizards are in the class Reptilia, and so the many classes are formed by the basic similarities between groups of animals. There are higher groups that bring the classes together, but we need to consider only the ranks lower than the

A hedgehog has a very keen sense of smell, which assists it greatly in its search for food.

class. Mammals are divided into 21 orders. Some examples are: Carnivora—the flesh eaters—dogs, cats, bears, raccoons, and their like; Primates—monkeys, apes, and man; and Chiroptera—bats. Our subjects, hedgehogs, are in the order Insectivora, the insect eaters.

Orders are divided into families. In Carnivora, there is Felidae, the cats; Canidae, the dogs; Ursidae, the bears—and so on. Insectivora is divided into seven families. Our interest lies in those called Erinaceidae and Tenrecidae, the hedgehogs and tenrecs. Families are divided into genera (singular: genus), and the genera are divided into species. A species is a group of individuals that share very many features in common and that will freely interbreed to produce fertile offspring of their own kind in their wild habitat. When a population of individuals within a species are separated by some physical barrier, such as a river, lake, sea, or mountain range, they will tend to develop features that progressively distinguish them from their root stock. They become a subspecies. Given sufficient time (thousands of years), they will become clearly distinct from their root stock. They may no longer interbreed with them even if the opportunity arises under natural conditions. They have become a full species. This is evolution in progress.

A species is identified by being given two names. One indicates the genus (generic name) that it belongs to; the other is a

Inspecting the nest of a newborn litter. These babies will not be handled until they are about three weeks of age.

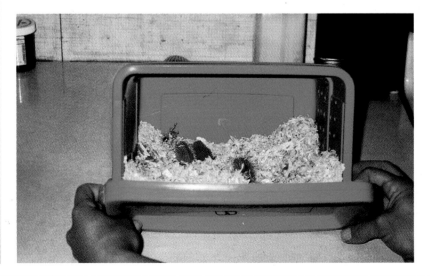

Hedgehogs do not have exotic food require-ments, just readily available items, in a wide variety.

descriptive term (the trivial, or specific, name). Only when used together do they uniquely identify that species. The binomial system uses Latin as the basic language, but Greek and Latinized words of other languages are also used. It is customary to print species' names in a typeface that differs from the main text typeface, which is why you will see that species names are nearly always printed in italics. The genus always commences with a capital letter; the trivial, or specific, name, always commences with a lower-case letter.

A subspecies is indicated by using a trinomial. How this works is that the original form identified as a species is called the nominate race. Its trivial name is repeated to indicate that it is the original form recognized. Thus the nominate form of the long-eared desert hedgehog, which has the species name of *Hemiechinus auritus,* became *Hemiechinus auritus auritus* once a subspecies was accepted. The subspecies became *Hemiechinus auritus megalotis,* the Afghan long-eared desert hedgehog.

The binomial system may seem complex to the newcomer, compounded by the fact that Latin is used, this being a strange language to the average person. But once the basics are understood, it is actually a very practical system. It is accepted in all countries of the world. The name *Erinaceus europaeus* is instantly identified as the European hedgehog regardless of whether a person lives in

China, the US, France, or Russia. The same is so of all other living organisms, each having its own quite unique binomial name. There is, of course, a lot more to learn about taxonomy, but that which is detailed here gives you the fundamentals of the system so that you are not mystified why these sometimes-cumbersome names are used.

At the top of the system is the rank of kingdom. It includes all living organisms recognized as being animals. Their single affinity is that they are living creatures (as opposed to being plants or non-living objects like rocks). The system then fans out like a pyramid. On the base line are all the individual species—over one million of them. By having the series of ranks between the kingdom and the species, you can relate to specific groups of animals without the need to mention the many members by name.

COMMON NAMES

A species may have no common name, or it may have many. Such names will also differ in each language. Unlike the carefully administrated application of scientific names, there are no rules or guidelines where common names are used.

Any person is free to call a given species whatever he chooses to. Only by regular use, thus convention, might a common name have widely accepted status within a given country.

A number of hedgehog species have no common names but are simply known as hedgehogs. They may be given a group common name, such as desert hedgehogs or long-eared hedgehogs, but none of these terms are specific to a single species. In the following text, I have applied a common name to every species, including those for which I could find no common name already in use within scientific texts. While common names do have practical-use advantages, it is strongly advised that you should be familiar with the correct scientific species, and even subspecies, name of the pet that you purchase if it can be ascertained with some degree of certainty. If you become a breeder, this approach will make obtaining members of the same species much easier than if you use common names. In the following text, only a single species from each genus is detailed. This is because, in hedgehogs, differences between species of a given genus are often very minor and based on cranial or dental variations that are not readily apparent unless the individual is carefully studied and measurements taken of skull width and length, of teeth structure, and so on. (The listing is after Walker 1991.)

FAMILY ERINACEIDAE

Genus *Erinaceus:*
Eurasian hedgehogs
13-30 cm; tail 1-5cm

There are five digits on each foot. The color of the spines, which are smooth, are normally a dark brown tipped with yellow; but this is variable, and some appear almost black. Others may be very light colored. The face and underparts, which are covered with soft fur, are light brown or gray-white. The muzzle is often a darker color than the surrounding fur. The

A wild hedgehog exploring its territory for food.

Erinaceus europaeus: European hedgehog

This is the common hedgehog of Great Britain, France, Germany, and other West European countries. It may weigh anything from 14-40 oz. (400-1120g). The snout is elongate and pointed, though not as apparently so as in some other genera.

spines commence on the crown of the head just forward of the short erect ears. The female has five pairs of mammae. She may give birth to one or two litters in a year, with the breeding period being from late April through October. The gestation period is 31 to 36 days, and the litter range is two to seven, with three to four being typical. Longevity is recorded as being about seven years, both in the wild and under captive conditions. The sexes are solitary except during the brief mating period. The species does not appear to be territorial in the wild, but may certainly be so under captive conditions where space is restricted. Other species in the genus are: *E.concolor*

(Eurasian hedgehog), and *E.amurensis* (Amur hedgehog).

Genus *Atelerix:* African hedgehogs

17-24cm; tail 1.5-5cm

Atelerix albiventris: African pygmy hedgehog (sometimes also referred to as the dwarf hedgehog, pygmy hedgehog, African hedgehog, or white-bellied hedgehog)

This species is somewhat smaller than its European cousin, but this is a relative state and therefore not always a reliable identification guide. More noteworthy is that it invariably has only four toes on its hind feet. If a fifth toe or hallux is present, it is greatly reduced in size. Visually, members of the genus are similar in color to *Erinaceus*, though the base of the spines, and the tips, are usually white rather than yellow-brown. Other

differences between the two genera, other than mentioned, and within genus members, are related to the cranium and the teeth. The underbelly fur ranges from almost white to very dark brown or even black.

The female has five pairs of mammae. The breeding period (in the wild) is October to March. The gestation period is 32-36 days. The litter range is one to ten, with four to five being typical. Sexual maturity is attained at around eight to ten weeks of age, this being only two or so weeks after youngsters have been weaned from their mother. Longevity records are scant, but five to seven years may be assumed typical under good conditions of care.

Other species in the genus are: *A. sclateri* (Sclater's hedgehog), *A. frontalis* (South African hedgehog), and *A. algirus* (Algerian hedgehog). *A. frontalis* is now cited as a threatened species in South Africa and appears on the Cites 2 list.

It should be noted that in some texts, you may find *Atelerix* being treated as a subgenus of *Erinaceus*. Also, *A. frontalis* and *A. algirus* are upgraded to the generic rank of *Aethechinus* by some authorities. These matters are subjective to those zoologists who prepare classifications. They are mentioned so that you are aware that these species may not always carry the same generic name, but the trivial name is retained.

The species *A. albiventris* is, of course, the one that has emerged as the "new pet" of the 1990s and that

wavy, rather than smooth) spines are banded in brown, black, and white or yellow. Some examples show quite strong melanistic tendencies so they may appear almost brown-black. At the other extreme, individuals appear a very light brown to almost yellow. The mask is equally variable, from almost black to very light

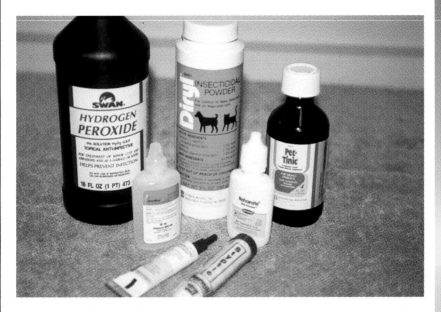

The pet owner's first aid kit should be acquired with the help of a veterinarian before any problem arises.

prompted the writing of this book.

Genus *Paraechinus:* desert hedgehogs
14-28cm; tail 1-4cm
Paraechinus aethiopicus: North African desert hedgehog

Smaller than the European hedgehog, members of this genus are also more consistently variable in their coloration. The rugose (wrinkled or

brown. The sides and underbelly may be brown patches on a white background, all white-gray, or all light brown.

The desert hedgehogs appear to possess specialized kidneys that allow them to survive for a few weeks without water, but this is certainly not recommended with captive specimens. Members of the genera are probably somewhat more insectivorous than other genera in the sense that they consume less vegetable matter. *P. micropus* is said to store food in its burrow and eats no plant matter.

Litter size is in the range of one to six, with one to two being typical of *P. micropus*, and three to four being typical of *P. hypomelas*. A captive individual of *P. aethiopicus* is recorded as having lived for $4^1/_2$ years, but it can be assumed that longevity may well exceed this. If one looks at zoological records of 20-30 years ago, it will be found that present-day lifespans are better. This is to be expected once any wild species starts to become well established under captive conditions and begins the long process towards domestication.

Other species in the genus are: *P. hypomelas* (desert hedgehog) and *P. micropus* (Asiatic dwarf desert hedgehog).

Genus *Hemiechinus*: long-eared hedgehogs
15-28cm; tail 1-5.5cm
Hemiechinus auritus: long-eared desert hedgehog
The obvious feature of these hedgehogs is that the ears are larger than in the other genera. This species, whose ears help to dissipate heat, is more adapted to hot zones. The species lacks the short spineless tract that is seen on the crown of the other genera. The underparts are usually white or gray. Like the other desert genera species, those of this genus have also evolved to go quite long periods—a number of weeks—without either food or water. However, this would   not be good for their general health, so the situation should never arise under captive conditions. The gestation period is 35-44 days and the litter range one to seven. Captive individuals have lived for nearly seven years.

It is reported that long-eared hedgehogs are less tractable than *Atelerix* (based on a few importations into the US) and therefore are unsuitable as pets. However, this author would question such a comment based on so few individuals.

FAMILY TENRECIDAE
Genus *Tenrec*
26-40cm; tail 1-1.6cm
Tenrec ecaudatus: tenrec or common Madagascar "hedgehog"
The largest of the "hedgehogs," this species, like the streaked tenrec, is quite distinct from all others. For one thing, its coat is not totally covered with spines but is a

mixture of stiff hairs and spines. The spines are not as sharp as those in other hedgehogs. Down the back, they are longer than elsewhere on the body. When threatencd, thc long hairs are raised to make the tenrec look larger than it really is. It does not roll into a ball, as is typical of hedgehogs. The general

This makes the species one of the most prolific producers of offspring per litter of any mammal. The gestation period is about 55-65 days. As with most hedgehogs, the species is very much a "loner,"other than for the breeding period. Longevity is recorded at about six to seven years.

Inspect your hedgehog's nails regularly. Clipping can be done with human nail clippers. Keep a styptic pencil handy in case of minor bleeding.

color is shades of brown to red, this being variable as it is in all hedgehogs. The underbelly is a lighter color. The digits, as in the "true" hedgehogs, are five and five. The snout is long and very slender. The ears are short.

The female has no less than 12 pairs of mammae, which suggests large litter sizes. This is, in fact, the case. The range is 1-32, with 12-16 being typical.

Genus *Setifer*
15-22cm; tail 1.5cm
Setifer setosus: setifer or large Madagascar "hedgehog"

The setifer has the appearance of the European hedgehog but is rather smaller and somewhat longer. Its coat is tightly packed with spines that range in color from a light to dark brown, this being determined by the extent of white tipping to the spines. The whiskers on the face are longer and more obvious than in other hedgehogs. The underbelly may be dark or light brown, or gray-white. The facial mask also varies from dark to light, depending on the individual.

The female has five pairs of mammae. The gestation period ranges from 51-69 days and is apparently influenced by the ambient temperature. It is shorter when it is warmer. The litter range is one to five, with two to three being typical. Longevity is quite good under captive conditions, with $10^1/_2$ years having been documented.

Genus *Hemicentetes*
16-17cm; tail vestigial
Hemicentetes semispinosus: streaked tenrec

This is the most aberrant form of hedgehog in many ways. It is instantly recognized by its coloration. This comprises a ground color of black on which there are white or brown streaks of various lengths in a longitudinal manner on the body. Around the neck, there is a very obvious ruff of long spines in white or brown; these colors are also seen on the underparts, according to the subspecies. The mask is black, and the snout is long.

The coat is a mixture of soft to harsh fur interspersed with very sharp spines, which are also found on the underbelly in the subspecies *H. s. semispinosus*. The spines give the impression of those on a cactus. When threatened, this tenrec, like the common tenrec, does not curl into a ball. Instead it lowers its snout, spreads the spines on its nape, and thrusts upward in a bull-like manner!

The gestation period is 55-63 days, and the litter range is two to four or two to eleven, according to the subspecies (which some authorities regard as separate species). Another very unusual feature of these fascinating creatures is that they are quite social. Groups of ten or more individuals, probably families, have been seen together. Lengthy communal burrows have also been seen, which are never excavated by any of the other hedgehog-like genera. It would seem, however, that this species is possibly the shortest-lived of the hedgehogs, at least under captive conditions. The longest-recorded lifespan appears to be only 31 months.

Genus *Echinops*
14-15cm; tail absent
Echinops telfairi: small Madagascar "hedgehog"

The smallest of the "hedgehogs," this species differs from the setifer in that it has no tail, is smaller, and has only 32 teeth compared to the 36 of the setifer. In coloration, it is similar to the setifer and other hedgehog-like mammals. The spines are dense and project out at all angles to the body, making a formidable barrier for would-be predators to penetrate. It is unusual in that it is the only typical-looking "hedgehog" that appears to tolerate its conspecifics (own kind) other than during the breeding period. Mated pairs may remain together for lengthy periods, as might females. But this social tolerance does not appear to extend to males, which will fight aggressively in each other's company, and especially when a potential breeding female is nearby.

The gestation period is 42-49 days, and the litter range is one to ten with four to six being typical. The species has done well in captivity in respect to longevity. The oldest individual attained 13 years of age, a goodly lifespan for any animal of this of size.

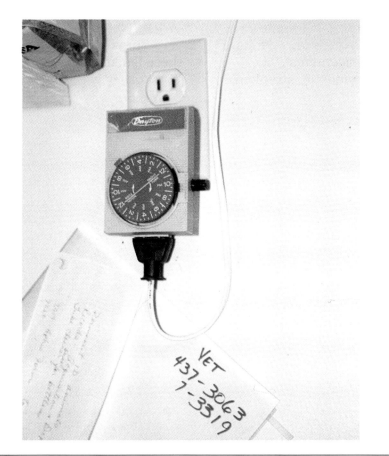

Breeders must pay careful attention to duplicating a "springtime" environment. Here, a timer controls the daylight-simulating light source for a consistent 12-hour period of light.

The North American Hedgehog Association is committed to educating new owners

about the proper care of these fascinating little animals.

North American Hedgehog Association

It is always important that when a new pet arrives on the scene, it should have a national club devoted to it. This serves a number of purposes:

1. It provides a source of reference on all aspects of management for breeders and owners.

2. It provides a single means through which hobbyists can unite in order to fight legislation that may often be based on incorrect (or no) facts about the species in question.

3. It enables breeders to pool and disseminate their collective knowledge so that the hobby can expand to the benefit of all involved in it.

4. It provides the means for breeder registration.

5. Through its administration, shows, and educational leaflets, it is able to promote and represent the hobby.

The NAHA was the first and remains the only club devoted to these fascinating pets. It is, therefore, appropriate that its brief history and objectives be documented as an integral part of the developing hobby history.

A BRIEF PRE-NAHA HISTORY

Hedgehogs have been imported into the US for very many years.

The New York Zoological Society obtained a female as far back as 1900 and housed other specimens of *Erinaceus europaeus* in later years, as did the National Zoological Park, Washington. The New York Zoo imported a specimen of *Hemiechinus auritus auritus* (the long-eared hedgehog) from Cyprus in 1946. There has been a trickle flow of different species since those days. However, the hedgehog is not actually the most exciting zoological exhibit, so it is not surprising that it was little known to the public at large in the US. Breeding records were and remain sparse in zoos; indeed, most zoos were not very successful in keeping these insectivores alive for more than a few years until more recent times.

In recent years, a few hedgehogs had been imported as exotic novelties, but no concerted efforts to establish breeding lines appear to have taken place until Pat Storer, and more recently Ralph and Laura Lermayer, and LaDonna Stage began them. Pat Storer, at her Country Storer Ranch in Texas, obtained specimens from zoos and private collectors, building up a herd of about 25 individuals. She also began importing specimens from Africa and is to be credited for conducting what was probably the first large-scale, controlled pet-hedgehog breeding program in the US.

The Lermayers were to follow and gathered stock from around the nation, including from Alaska—of all places! They established seven breeding lines. Other breeders were, by 1990, beginning to establish small herds. It became clear that these little animals were destined to have a bright future. In 1991, Pat Storer wrote and privately published the first book on these animals as pets, thus giving further recognition to the hedgehog hobby.

NAHA IS FORMED

By 1993, a number of breeders had produced hedgehogs to at least the fifth generation, but no specialist club devoted to these pets had been started. Indeed, their status as pets was still unclear in many states. In order to address the need, Ralph Lermayer, together with Albuquerque attorney Rod Frechette, owner of the Hedgehog Haven herd in Corrales, New Mexico, decided to finance and create an incorporated association. The NAHA was born, with Ralph and Rod as its co-founder directors.

A small inaugural meeting of interested breeders and hobbyists took place in Denver, Colorado, on April 22, 1993. Among those who were present were the following: Bonnie Bogart, Julie Bowers, Rod and Michelle Frechette, Ralph and Laura Lermayer, Larry Lorenzen, Pat Storer, Darla Taylor, and Neil Teddington. As a consequence of this meeting, a breeder registry was started; and a newsletter, *The Hedgehog News,* was issued shortly afterward. This was well presented and carried articles of importance to hedgehog owners. Since the first issue, others have followed.

One of the NAHA's first tasks was to address the status of the hedgehog in the US. Meetings were arranged with USDA officials and questionnaires sent to all states to clarify the situation. As a direct result of the NAHA's efforts, more states now accept the

The NAHA provides a forum through which hedgehog breeders can share their knowledge and experience for the betterment of the hobby.

hedgehog than was the case before the association was formed. Although it is unusual for a national hobby association, the NAHA is actively seeking ways in which to work closely with the pet industry to ensure that only well-bred and tractable individuals are sold as pets.

Recognizing the fact that the window to all animal-hobby pursuits is the exhibition side of a pet, the NAHA is at this time actively researching a range of show systems in order to establish which is felt to be the most appropriate for this particular pet.

As with any new association, the onward success of the NAHA will be dependent on the support its receives from those in the hobby.

Whether your interest in hedgehogs is as a single-companion pet, as a breeder, or as an exhibitor, you now have the vehicle to channel that interest into helping to shape the future of these fascinating little animals. Any new national association faces enormous administrative and planning problems, but it is not very often that the opportunity comes for new hobbyists to involve themselves in this area. So, if it appeals to you, you should become an active member of your association. Even if you live outside of the US, the NAHA will welcome you as a member. Address your inquiries to: North American Hedgehog Association, Inc., 601 Tijeras NW-Suite 201, Albuquerque, NM, 87102.

NAHA members pictured at their initial meeting in Denver, Colorado.

References

Although it is not customary in popular pet books to list numerous scientific references, the author felt that in view of the lack of books devoted to the hedgehog species, it would be advantageous to do so. It is hoped that this will save the serious hobbyist laborious time in researching such references. The listing is selective.

Brockie, R. 1974. Self-anointing in wild hedgehogs, *Erinaceus europaeus*, in *New Zealand Animal Behavior*, 24:68-71

Brodie, E. D., Brodie, E. D. Jr., & Johnson, A. J. 1982. Breeding the African Hedgehog *Atelerix Pruneri* in Captivity. *International Zoo Yearbook*, 22: 195-197

Brodie, E. D. Jr. 1977. Hedgehogs use toad venom in their own defense. *Nature*, 268: 627-628

Boitani, L. & Reggiani, G. 1984. Movements and activity patterns in hedgehogs (*Erinaceus europaeus*) in Mediterranean coastal habitats. Z. Saugetierk. 49:193-206

Corbet, G. B. 1988. The family Erinaceidae: a synthesis of taxonomy, phylogeny, ecology, and zoogeography. *Mammalian Review*. 18:117-72

Crandall, Lee S. 1964. *The Management of Wild Animals in Captivity*, pp 46-48, University of Chicago Press, Chicago and London

Jones, M. L. 1982. Longevity of captive animals, *Zoo Garten*, 52:113-28

Mayr, Ernst 1969. *Principles of Systematic Zoology*, McGraw-Hill Co., New York and London

NAHA 1993, 1994. *The Hedgehog News*, No. 1, (1993) No. 2, (1994) Albuquerque, New Mexico

Nowak, Ronald M. 1991. *Walker's Mammals of the World*, Fifth edition, Vol. 1, pp 114-137, Johns Hopkins University Press, Baltimore and London

Robins, C. B. & Setzer, H. W. 1985. Morphometrics and distinctiveness of the hedgehog genera (Insectivora: Erinaceidae), *Proc. Biol. Soc.*, Washington, 98:112-120

Schoenfeld, M. & Yom-tov, Y. 1985. The biology of two species of hedgehogs, *Erinaceus europaeus concolor* and *Hemiechinus auritus aegypticus*, in Israel,

Mammalia, 49:339-355

Storer, Pat 1994. *Everything You Wanted To Know About Hedgehogs But You Didn't Know Who To Ask.* Third edition, Country Storer Enterprises, Columbus, Texas

Walton, G. M. & Walton, D. W. 1973. Notes on hedgehogs of the lower Indus Valley, *Korean Journ. Zoo.,* 16: 161-170

Zaitsev, M. V. 1984. A contribution to the taxonomy and diagnostics of the subgenus *Erinaceus* (Mammalia, Erinaceini) of the fauna of the USSR, *Zool. Zhur.* 63:720-730.

This weaning pen affords ample space and visibility for young hedgehogs.

This pair of hedgehogs is being shipped by air. The cardboard tube in each compartment will provide a good hiding place and will help to lessen the stress of travel.

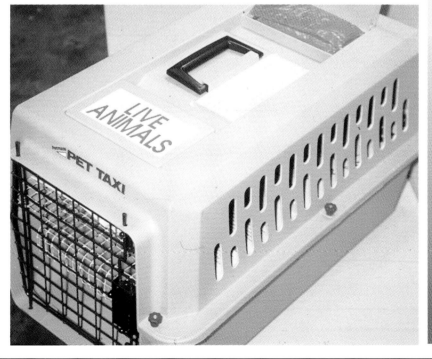

Any type of carrier that you select for your hedgehog must provide adequate ventilation.

Index

In addition to books about hedgehogs, T.F.H. Publications offers a comprehensive selection of books dealing with various other small mammals. A selection of significant titles is presented below; they and many other works are available from your local pet shop.

TS-181

TW-108

TU-014

KW-074

TU-006

CO-038S

TT-008

SK-011

TU-002

TW-106

SK-040

TT-006

TT-019

KW-224

T-107

E-724

PB-124

KW-021